# DIY Guide to Forming your Own LLC

A Detail Step By Step Guide to Starting & Filing a Limited Liability Company For All 50 States & DC

By

**Aaron Sanders**

Copyright © 2018 – **Lost River Publishing House**

All Rights Reserved.

*No part of this publication may be reproduced, stored in a retrieval system or transmitted in any form or by any means, electronic, mechanical, photocopying, recording or otherwise without the proper written consent of the copyright holder, except as permitted under Sections 107 & 108 of the 1976 United States Copyright Act, without the prior written permission of the publisher.*

*Lost River Publishing House publishes its books and guides in a variety of electronic and print formats. Some content that appears in print may not be available in electronic format, and vice versa.*

Cover design

Robin Goodnight

*First Edition*

# TABLE OF CONTENTS

Foreword .................................................................................. 8
**Part -1** ................................................................................... 9
**How to Start Your Own LLC** ............................................... 9
Introduction - The Basics ...................................................... 10
   What is an LLC? .................................................................. 10
   5 Key Advantages of Forming an LLC ................................ 11
      Run Your Own Business ................................................... 11
      Limit Liability ...................................................................... 12
      Better Taxes ....................................................................... 12
      Less Paperwork ................................................................. 13
      Profit Sharing Flexibility ..................................................... 13
   What Does an LLC Protect ................................................. 13
      The Exceptions .................................................................. 14
Structuring Your New LLC ..................................................... 17
   LLC Management Structures .............................................. 17
   Properly Documenting Your Structure ................................ 19
   LLC Member Duties & Responsibilities ............................. 20
      Duty of Loyalty .................................................................. 21
      Duty of Care ...................................................................... 22
      Changing Duties ................................................................ 22
      Member-Managed Fiduciary Duties ................................. 23
      Manager-Managed Duties ................................................ 23
Steps to Starting an LLC ....................................................... 25
   Operating Agreement ......................................................... 25
   The Importance of an Operating Agreement ...................... 26
      Protecting Limited Liability Status ..................................... 26
      Defining Business Structure ............................................. 27
      Overriding State Laws ...................................................... 27
   What's In an Operating Agreement .................................... 28
      Percentage of Interests .................................................... 29

> Distribution of Shares ............................................................. 29
> Distributing Profits and Losses ............................................... 30
> Member Voting Rights ............................................................ 31
> Transition of Ownership .......................................................... 32

How to Write an Operating Agreement ........................................ 32
Articles of Incorporation ................................................................ 33
> LLC Name ................................................................................ 34
> Registered Agent ..................................................................... 34
> Statement of Purpose .............................................................. 35
> LLC Management ..................................................................... 35
> Place of Business .................................................................... 36
> Business Duration .................................................................... 36
> Authorized Signatures ............................................................. 36
> Sample Articles of Incorporation ............................................. 37

Funding an LLC .............................................................................. 44
> Own Assets .............................................................................. 44
> Informal Loans ......................................................................... 44
> Additional Members ................................................................. 45
> Credit Cards ............................................................................. 45
> Conventional Loans ................................................................. 46
> Government Grants and Loans ............................................... 47
> Peer-to-Peer Lending Sites ..................................................... 47

Choosing a Fiscal Year .................................................................. 48
> Calendar Tax Year ................................................................... 48
> Fiscal Tax Year ........................................................................ 49
> Single Member LLC ................................................................. 50
> Partnership ............................................................................... 50
> Corporation .............................................................................. 50
> EIN From IRS ........................................................................... 52

Opening a Business Bank Account ............................................... 54
> Why Get a Business Bank Account ........................................ 54
> Documents You Will Need ...................................................... 55
> Opening An Account ................................................................ 55
> Types of Commercial Accounts .............................................. 57
> Other Key Factors ................................................................... 57

Registered Agent ..................................................................... 58
Running an LLC ........................................................................ 60
    Record Keeping Rules .......................................................... 60
        Documents of Organization ............................................. 61
        Financial and Tax Documents .......................................... 63
    Annual Reports ..................................................................... 65
    Meetings ................................................................................ 68
        Meeting Requirements ..................................................... 69
        Member Consent in Place of Meetings ............................. 70
        Why Hold Meetings ........................................................... 70
    How LLCs Are Taxed ............................................................ 71
        Income Taxes .................................................................... 71
        Single-Owner/Member LLCs ............................................. 72
        Multi-Owner/Member LLCs ............................................... 72
        IRS Form 1065 .................................................................. 72
        Electing Corporate Taxation .............................................. 73
    Estimating and Paying Income Taxes ................................... 74
    Self-Employment Taxes ......................................................... 75
    Deductions and Expenses ..................................................... 76
    State Fees and Taxes ............................................................ 77

**Part -2 ...................................................................................... 79**
**State by State Guide to Forming an LLC ......................... 79**
Alabama ....................................................................................... 80
Alaska .......................................................................................... 82
Arizona ......................................................................................... 85
Arkansas ...................................................................................... 87
California ..................................................................................... 89
Colorado ...................................................................................... 91
Connecticut ................................................................................. 93
Delaware ...................................................................................... 95
District of Columbia ................................................................... 97
Florida .......................................................................................... 99
Georgia ....................................................................................... 101
Hawaii ......................................................................................... 103

| | |
|---|---|
| Idaho | 105 |
| Illinois | 107 |
| Indiana | 109 |
| Iowa | 111 |
| Kansas | 113 |
| Kentucky | 115 |
| Louisiana | 117 |
| Maine | 119 |
| Maryland | 121 |
| Massachusetts | 123 |
| Michigan | 125 |
| Minnesota | 127 |
| Mississippi | 129 |
| Missouri | 131 |
| Montana | 133 |
| Nebraska | 136 |
| Nevada | 138 |
| New Hampshire | 140 |
| New Jersey | 142 |
| New Mexico | 144 |
| New York | 146 |
| North Carolina | 148 |
| North Dakota | 150 |
| Ohio | 152 |
| Oklahoma | 154 |
| Oregon | 156 |
| Pennsylvania | 158 |
| Rhode Island | 160 |
| South Carolina | 162 |
| South Dakota | 164 |
| Tennessee | 167 |
| Texas | 169 |
| Utah | 171 |
| Vermont | 173 |
| Virginia | 175 |
| Washington | 177 |
| West Virginia | 179 |

Wisconsin ............................................................................. 181
Wyoming ............................................................................. 183
CONCLUSION .................................................................... 186

# FOREWORD

This step by step guide is intended for people who are about to start a business and want to incorporate their venture for various protections and benefits that an LLC can offer. Incorporating your business not only gives you peace of mind but it offers a few very key benefits to your new business. Best of all, it is very simple to incorporate a business in the U.S and cost is very nominal too.

In this guide, I outlined every step you need to take to get started with incorporating your business. Since some of the requirements do vary widely from state to state, I included a step by step process which is easy to follow for all 50 states and District of Columbia including the most up to date filing costs for each states.

# PART -1

# HOW TO START YOUR OWN LLC

# INTRODUCTION - THE BASICS

An LLC or limited liability company provides protection from personal liability when it comes to business debts, similar to a corporation. Setting up an LLC is a little more difficult than a partnership or sole proprietorship, but running it is a lot easier.

This is why in this guide I'm going to walk you through all the steps you need to get your LLC up and running. Let's start by taking a brief look at what an LLC is and the basics behind it so you know why should set up an LLC.

## WHAT IS AN LLC?

A limited liability company is a business structure that makes it a separate entity from the owners, like the business structure of a corporation. However, an LLC is different from a corporation in the area of taxes.

A corporation needs to pay its own taxes while an LLC is a "pass-through" tax entity; meaning the profits and losses of the business pass on to the owners who report them on their personal tax returns just as in the structure of a partnership or sole proprietorship. Let's take a look at some of the advantages of an LLC so you can see why it is a good idea to start your own.

## 5 KEY ADVANTAGES OF FORMING AN LLC

If you are starting a new business, you should consider using the limited liability company structure since it offers key advantages that you don't get with other business structures. An LLC features many of the positive benefits of a sole proprietorship, partnership and corporation without many of the disadvantages. While state laws may vary for LLCs, most provide you with five main advantages.

### RUN YOUR OWN BUSINESS

If you prefer to do your own thing then structuring as a single member or owner LLC means you can be the sole owner. This means you are able to make all your own business decisions without needing to consult with and receive approval from other partners or a board of directors.

However, you don't have the same liability issues as a sole proprietor business. If you have two or more owners, you can also draft an operating agreement that shows the respective roles and obligations, so the business is structured in a way that best meets everyone's needs.

## LIMIT LIABILITY

An LLC is a separate legal entity from the individual members or business owners. This is similar to the shareholders of a corporation; meaning the LLC owner isn't personally liable for any debts or legal liabilities. You may still lose your capital contribution, but unlike sole proprietor or general partner businesses, you won't have to risk personal assets.

## BETTER TAXES

Most standard corporations face the issue of double income taxation; the profits are taxed as income and shareholders need to pay taxes on dividends. LLCs have a pass-through tax treatment in which profits are only taxed once on each member's individual income tax return.

## LESS PAPERWORK

Forming and running an LLC is not as complex as other businesses and doesn't require as much paperwork. An LLC registers by filing articles of organization and paying a fee to the relevant state office, typically the secretary of state. We'll discuss more about this later when we are talking about the steps of forming an LLC.

## PROFIT SHARING FLEXIBILITY

Most business structures distribute profits based on the capital contribution of the owner or the percentage of ownership interest. For a general partnership, profits are normally shared equally among partners.

For LLC members that is flexibility in how profits are allocated based on the operating agreement. LLC members are able to decide how they want to divide up their profits. The last thing we want to consider is just what an LLC protects you from; since this can also be considered one of their advantages.

# WHAT DOES AN LLC PROTECT

LLC owners are like shareholders in a corporation; they are protected from personal liability when it comes to business claims and debts. This means that if the business itself can't pay a creditor, then the creditor can't legally go after the owner's house, car or other personal possessions.

This means an LLC owner only stands to lose the money they've invested in a company if things don't work out. This is often known as the "limited liability" feature.

## THE EXCEPTIONS

While there is a lot of protection for LLC business owners, this isn't absolute. However, these same exceptions also apply to corporations. An LLC owner can still be found personally liable if they cause one of the following:

- Personally and directly cause injury to someone.
- Personally guarantees a bank loan or business debt that goes into default.
- Doesn't deposit taxes that are withheld from employees' wages.
- Purposefully doesn't something fraudulent, illegal or reckless that causes harm to the company or another individual.

- Treats the LLC as a part of their personal affairs rather than its own legal entity.

This last exception is perhaps the most important to understand when starting an LLC. You need to treat your LLC as a separate business otherwise a court can decide that your business doesn't really exist and that you are actually doing business as an individual who is personally responsible for your acts. To avoid this, you need to do the following:

- Act legally and fairly. Don't misrepresent or conceal the state of your finances or material facts to vendors, creditors or other non-business members.
- Adequately fund your LLC. Make sure you have enough cash invested in your business so that you can meet any reasonable expenses and liabilities.
- Keep your personal business separate from the LLC. Have a federal employer identification number, open a business only checking account and keep your personal finances separate.
- Have an operating agreement. Having this is formal writing can provide your LLC's separate existence with credibility. We'll discuss more about the operating agreement in detail later. For now,

let's move on to look at the structure of an LLC and how you should set up your business.

# STRUCTURING YOUR NEW LLC

The first thing you'll need to do when starting an LLC is to decide how the company will be managed. There are two different management structures to choose from when it comes to LLCs. There is a member-managed LLC where all the owners participate together in running the business.

The other option is a manager-managed LLC where only specific, designated members, or certain non-members/outsiders, or a combination of members and non-members are allowed the responsibility of running the business.

Under this structure, the other members are passive investors who don't become involved in the operations of the business. Let's look a little more closely at the two options available to help you decide which is right for your company.

## LLC MANAGEMENT STRUCTURES

Most people who are starting an LLC, choose to go with a member-management structure. This means that all members or owners of the LLC will share the day-to-day running and responsibilities for the business. This approach is most preferred because a lot of LLCs are small businesses that have limited resources and don't need to have a separate management level in order to operate.

LLCs are different from corporations in the fact that they have a more streamlined organization structure. This is because an LLC doesn't have officers or a board of directors. LLCs are often formed by individuals who want to be directly involved in operating and managing their business.

If you are this type of person and want to stay focused on making and selling products, taking orders or providing services; then you should choose a member-management structure for your LLC. In fact, in most states, LLCs are member-managed by default according to state law. This means that if you don't designate a management structure in formation documents or an operating agreement, then you will automatically be considered a member-managed organization.

However, there are still going to be times when a manager-management structure is preferred. This is best when some members of the company want nothing more than to be a passive investor in the business. These are the individuals who prefer to delegate management duties to other people or nonmembers. Some other situations where an LLC manager-management structure may be preferred include the following:

1. The business or ownership becomes too large, diverse or complex for management sharing among all owners.
2. When owners or members are skilled at management.

In both of these situations, delegating management to others can be the best way to balance the skills and interests of LLC members. It can also lead to better management of the business.

## PROPERLY DOCUMENTING YOUR STRUCTURE

You may not be required to formally document your LLC structure choice if you decide on member-management; although most states will ask that you state your LLC structure in the articles of organization that you file when forming your LLC. However, all LLCs should also have a written operating agreement that clearly states the basic rights and responsibilities of the members and managers.

If you choose a manager-management structure for your LLC, then you may face a legal requirement that you clearly state your choice in the LLCs organizational documents. This will often be in the articles of organization or your operating agreement.

If you don't create an operating agreement, then your states individual rules will apply. These may not be the rules you want for your business so you should make sure you have a written agreement for your LLC. To help you decide on a structure for your LLC, you should carefully consider the member duties of your company.

## LLC MEMBER DUTIES & RESPONSIBILITIES

When you are the manager or a member of an LLC, then you will owe duties of trust or fiduciary duties to the LLC. When it comes to an LLC, it is essential that you can rely upon and trust those who are in charge in order to manage the LLC and promote the best interest of the business. The fiduciary duty will depend on whether the LLC is member or manager managed and what level of management responsibilities LLC members have. An LLC is owed two key fiduciary duties:

1. The duty of loyalty
2. The duty of care

## DUTY OF LOYALTY

Under this duty, a manager or members need to put the success of and benefits to the LLC above any individual or personal advantages. When showing loyalty to the LLC, a person needs to act honestly in any dealings with the company and to avoid any conflicts of interest between the businesses objectives and their own goals.

Under this duty, an individual can't take advantage of any of the LLC businesses opportunities, accrue secret profits from the commercial activities of the business or directly compete with the business. In some instances, you can receive a benefit from the LLCs opportunities as long as you provide full disclosure to and gain approval from the LLC first.

## DUTY OF CARE

This duty requires members or owners to act in good faith and exercise reasonable care when it comes to their obligations to and directing the activities of the LLC. You are often not liable for business decisions made in good faith with reasonable care if they adversely impact the business as a result of the business judgment rule.

## CHANGING DUTIES

Most states have statutes or judicial decisions that spell out the fiduciary duties of LLC members. Some states don't allow these fiduciary duties to be restricted or eliminated by members or managers. Other states allow members or managers to change or eliminate fiduciary duties with a separate contract or under operating agreement terms that define the authority of members or managers when operating the LLC. It is best to discuss this with an attorney to make sure case law or statues in your state permit this.

## MEMBER-MANAGED FIDUCIARY DUTIES

LLC members can choose to participate in the management of an LLC. The members who operate the business owe the duties of loyalty and reasonable care to any non-managing LLC owners. Depending on your state you may be able to revise, broaden or eliminate these duties through a separate contract or under the operating agreement conditions.

## MANAGER-MANAGED DUTIES

LLC owners may also choose to delegate their duties to managing the LLC to an outside management that can be either a member or a non-owner of the business. In this case, the LLC owners who don't manage the company normally don't owe the duties to each other.

However, external managers that operate the business do need to comply with the fiduciary obligations. If your state allows, you can modify or remove these duties by separate control or under a provision included in the operating agreement.

Now that we have the basics out of the way. Let's look at some of the specifics of starting an LLC. We'll also discuss in detail the paperwork you need in order to get your LLC started.

# STEPS TO STARTING AN LLC

When it comes to starting an LLC there are four main things you need to consider:

1. The Operating Agreement
2. Articles of Incorporation
3. Start-Up Funds and Financial Obligations
4. Selecting a Registered Agent

Not all states will have these requirements. Let's look at what you need for each of these in detail, and at the end of this guidebook you can find out whether or not it is needed in your state.

## OPERATING AGREEMENT

The operating agreement allows an LLC to structure your financial and working relationships with co-workers in a way that works for your business. The operating agreement is also where you and your co-owners will establish a percentage of ownership, the share of profits and losses, rights and responsibilities and what happens to the business if an owner leaves. Let's look into what you specifically need for this document.

# THE IMPORTANCE OF AN OPERATING AGREEMENT

While there are quite a few states that don't require you to have an operating agreement to operate, it is an important document to have; even if you are the sole owner of the LLC. Let's look at why you should have this important document.

The operating agreement allows you to protect your limited liability status, prevent misunderstandings in financial and/or management areas, and to make sure your business is governed by your rules and not those created by your state.

## PROTECTING LIMITED LIABILITY STATUS

Perhaps the most important reasons for having an operating agreement is to ensure the courts respect the limited personal liability status of your company. This is extremely important with a one-person LLC where the LLC will look like a sole proprietorship without the formality of an operating agreement. An operating agreement will help with the credibility of the separate existence of your LLC.

## DEFINING BUSINESS STRUCTURE

If an LLC is co-owned, then you need to use the operating agreement to document the profit-sharing and decision-making protocols along with the procedures for what to do when members depart or come on board with the company. Without an operating agreement, LLC owners won't be able to settle misunderstandings when it comes to management and finances. Also, without an operating agreement, your LLC will need to follow the default operating rules under your state's laws.

## OVERRIDING STATE LAWS

Each state has their own basic operating rules or laws for LLCs. Some of these rules will determine how you govern your business unless you have an operating agreement that states otherwise. This is known as default rules.

For example, in most states, there is a default rule that owners must divide up LLC profits and losses equally no matter what investment a member made to the business.

If you didn't invest equally in the business then you probably don't want to share profits equally. In order to prevent this from happening your operating agreement needs to spell out specifically how profits and losses are split.

When you put together an operating agreement, you will be able to choose the rules that determine the inner workings of your LLC, rather than having to simply follow the default rules that may not be ideal for your LLC.

## WHAT'S IN AN OPERATING AGREEMENT

There are plenty of issues to include in an operating agreement for an LLC. Most of these issues will depend on the particular situation and needs of your business. Most LLC operating agreements need to include the following:

- The percentage interests of members in the LLC
- The rights and responsibilities of members
- The voting powers of members
- The allocation of profits and losses
- How the LLC is managed

- Rules for how meetings are held and how votes are taken
- Provisions for buyout or buy-sell if a member wants to sell their interest, dies or becomes disabled

While a lot of this may seem very simple and straightforward, a lot of these do require important decisions that need to be spelled out clearly in the operating agreement. Let's look at this each in greater detail.

## PERCENTAGE OF INTERESTS

Most LLC owners will make a financial contribution in cash, property or services in order to help the business get started. In return, each member gets a percentage of ownership in the LLC's assets. Members typically get a percentage in relation to the contributions of their capital, but the members are free to divide up ownership however they want. These percentages are important to spell out in the operating agreement.

## DISTRIBUTION OF SHARES

LLC owners receive ownership interests in exchange for their capital contributions. In addition, they also get shares in the profits and losses of the LLC, something is known as "distributive shares."

Operating agreements typically provide specifics on each owner's distributive share in relation to their percentage of ownership in the LLC. If the LLC wants to assign distributive shares that aren't the same as percentage interests in the LLC, then you'll need to follow the rules for "special allocations." This is something you should seek professional legal help for when drafting your operating agreement.

## DISTRIBUTING PROFITS AND LOSSES

In addition to defining the distributive share of each owner, the operating agreement also needs to answer three questions:

1. How much of the LLC's profits are to be distributed to members each year?
2. Does the LLC have to pay members at least enough to cover the income taxes they'll owe on the yearly allocation of LLC profits?
3. Are profits regularly distributed or do the owners draw at will from the business profits?

Each co-owner may have different financial needs and may even be in different tax brackets. This is why it is important you pay close attention to how you allocate profits and losses. It may also be a good idea to run this part of your operating agreement by a tax professional in order to make sure you are getting the financial results you want.

## MEMBER VOTING RIGHTS

Often LLC management decisions are made on an informal basis; other times the decision may be so important or controversial that it is essential to have a formal vote first. There are two main ways to divide the voting power among members of an LLC:

1. The voting power of each member corresponds to their percentage interest in the LLC, or
2. Each member gets a single vote known as "per capita" voting.

Most LLCs choose to have votes be in proportion to the ownership interests. No matter what method you choose, you want to specify in your operating agreement just how much voting power a member has along with whether or not a majority of votes or a unanimous decision is needed in order to settle an issue.

### TRANSITION OF OWNERSHIP

When you're starting a new business, the last thing on your mind is what you will do if an owner retires, dies or decides to sell their interest in the company. All operating agreements should include a section on buyout options or rules for what happens should a member leave an LLC for any reason.

## HOW TO WRITE AN OPERATING AGREEMENT

Obviously you are going to need help drafting your operating agreement beyond the information provided above. The best option is to hire a professional to help you draft the contents. Otherwise, take a look online at websites such as Nolo.com, and you can find a blank template to help walk you through the process. Once you have a handle on your operating agreement, it's time to consider another important document: the articles of incorporation.

# Articles of Incorporation

When you choose to start an LLC, the first formal step you'll likely take is to file a special document with a particular office in your state. In most states, this document is called the articles of incorporation or articles of organization. Often this document is filed with the Secretary of State.

However, each state may have a different name or a different office where it needs to be filed. At the end of this guide, you can find this specific information in our State Guide. For now, let's look at the details of this simple form that is so important to the formation of your LLC.

While this document may vary slightly among states, the following pieces of information are typically needed for the articles of incorporation:

- The LLC name
- The LLC's registered agent including name and address
- A statement about the purpose of the LLC
- How the LLC will be managed

- The principal place of business address for the LLC
- The duration of the LLC
- One or more authorized signatures

## LLC Name

This part of the document may seem simple. However, you first need to make sure the name you are providing doesn't conflict with the name of any pre-existing business that is already registered in the state. If you LLC name shares that of another business then your filing will be rejected. To avoid this, you need to search business names already registered in your state. You can often do this through the Secretary of State's website.

## Registered Agent

This is a person who you designate to receive any official papers on behalf of your LLC. This can include renewal notices and any other key communications from the state, particularly those related to lawsuits. A registered agent needs to be located within the state where your LLC is organized, and you need to have a physical address for the registered agent.

Often a registered agent will be a member of the LLC and the address will be that of the business location. Other times you may choose to appoint a specific individual like a lawyer to act on behalf of the company as a registered agent. We'll look at this area in greater detail a little later.

## STATEMENT OF PURPOSE

A lot of states don't require you to have a specific purpose for your LLC. Rather you often just need a statement to the effect of: "The purpose of the Limited Liability Company is to engage in any lawful activity for which a Limited Liability Company may be organized in this state."

The only exception to this rule is if you are forming a professional limited liability company; then you'll need to be more specific about the type of professional services your business will provide.

## LLC MANAGEMENT

As we discussed before, LLCs can be managed either by members or by separate managers. Most states do require you to state which type of management is going to be used for your LLC. In a few states, you may also need to provide the names and addresses for managers.

## PLACE OF BUSINESS

This is nothing more than the main location of your business. For most small business, there will only be one location.

## BUSINESS DURATION

This is the length of time in years that the LLC plans to operate. Not all states will ask for this information and those that do ask for it, don't require you to have a specific answer. Rather the duration can simply be perpetual.

Actually, in many states, the default assumption is perpetual if you don't state a specific duration. Although in some states there is a statutory limit on the duration. These limits are often several decades in length, at the end of which the term can be extended if the LLC is still in business.

## AUTHORIZED SIGNATURES

States often require at least one owner of the LLC to sign and date the articles of incorporation. For a member-managed LLC, you may want to have all members sign the articles to prove participation in the business.

Preparing and filing these articles of incorporation is only one of many steps when forming an LLC. There are going to be other initial tasks as well. For further information for your state, take a look at our state guide at the end of this book. Next, let's look at the financial aspect of starting an LLC.

SAMPLE ARTICLES OF INCORPORATION

STATE OF ALABAMA:
COUNTY OF SHELBY:

## ARTICLES OF ORGANIZATION
## OF
## R&B Auto Brokers LLC

The undersigned, acting as organizers of the R&B Auto Brokers LLC under the Alabama Limited Liability Company Act, adopt the following Articles of Organization for said Limited Liability Company.

## Article I
## Name of the Company

The name of the limited liability company is R&B Auto Brokers LLC (the "Company").

## Article II
## Period of Duration

The period of duration is ninety (90) years from the date of filing of these Articles of Organization with the Alabama Secretary of State, unless the Company is sooner dissolved.

## Article III

## Purpose of the Company

The Company is organized to engage in all legal and lawful purpose of Automobile wholesale business.

## Article IV
## Registered Office and Agent

The Company's registered office is at address is 123 Main Court, Birmingham, Alabama 35561; and the name and the address of the Company's initial registered agent is John Doe, 123 Main Court, Birmingham, Alabama 35561.

## Article V
## Members of the Organization

There is one (1) member, all of which are identified in the Exhibit A attached hereto and a part hereof. The initial capital contribution agreed to be made by both members are also listed on Exhibit A. The members have not agreed to make any additional contributions, but may agree to do so in the future upon the terms and conditions as set forth in the Operating Agreement.

## Article VI

## Additional Members

The members, as identified in the Company's Operating Agreement, reserve the right to admit additional members and determine the Capital Contributions of such Members. Notwithstanding the foregoing, the additional Members may not become managing unless and until selected to such position as provided in Article VII of the Company's Operating Agreement.

## Article VII
## Contribution upon Withdrawal of Members

The members shall have the right to continue the company upon the death, retirement, resignation, expulsion, bankruptcy or dissolution of a member or occurrence of any event which terminates the continued membership of a member in the Company (collectively, "Withdrawal"), as long as there is at least One remaining member, and the remaining member agree to continue the Company by unanimous written consent within 90 days after the Withdrawal of a Member, as set forth in the Operating Agreement of the Company.

## Article VIII

## Manager

The name and business address of the initial manager is:

John Doe

R&B Auto Brokers LLC
123 Main Court
Birmingham, Alabama 35561

The manager may be removed and replaced by the Members as provided in the Operating Agreement.

IN WITNESS WHEREOF, the undersigned have caused these Articles of Organization to be executed this ................ Day of ........................... 2018

_____          _____

R&B Auto Brokers LLC                 DATE

AN ALABAMA CORPORATION
BY: John Doe
ITS: Managing Member

This instrument prepared by:

Jane Doe
999 Super Ct
Birmingham, AL 35561

# EXHIBIT A

| MEMBERS | INTIAL CONTRIBUTION | INTEREST |
|---------|---------------------|----------|
| John Doe | Future Services Rendered | 100% |

# FUNDING AN LLC

An important part of starting a successful LLC is to have proper funding. The main reason most new businesses fail is that they don't have the necessary capital to move beyond the initial start-up phase.

An essential first step is to have an effective and detailed business plan to help you raise the funds you need. This will help illustrate your business to potential investors and prove to your lenders your ability to pay back loans or to gain profitability. There are several ways that you can fund your LLC. Let's look at some of the major ones.

## OWN ASSETS

The first place you should look is at your own personal assets and see if you can liquidate them or use them as collateral for loans. Perhaps you have equity in your home that can allow you to get a home equity loan to help finance your business.

## INFORMAL LOANS

Nearly anyone who has thought of starting a business has likely shared their idea with other friends and family members. Your strongest personal connections are likely going to be those in your social circle.

Those who know you best are also more likely to place their trust and cash behind your start-up business. While these informal loans can be easy to get, beware of any issues they can pose to family and friend relationships if something goes wrong.

## ADDITIONAL MEMBERS

Bringing aboard other members can be another way to fund your start-up LLC. While you may want to be a single owner, consider the value of adding other LLC members when it comes to funding purposes. You will be able to pool your financial resources with other members, and this can also help to widen your network of business contacts and other investors. New members can also potentially help add professional experience to your company.

## CREDIT CARDS

Some individuals decide to start their business with personal credit cards. Many card companies also offer business credit cards that have low to no annual fees, good interest rates and travel rewards and/or cash back depending on the type of business purchases you make.

Credit cards off your immediate credit without all the paperwork of a loan application. However, most credit cards only offer short-term financial solutions for LLC and should be paid back as soon as possible. Avoid extending credit card debt for too long otherwise; it could become more costly.

## CONVENTIONAL LOANS

The traditional financing route is to seek out loans from a bank or credit union. For this option, you will need a formal business plan. Most conventional lenders are careful of funding inexperienced business people so be prepared for a lot of rejection at first. You can improve your chance of getting financed by borrowing against existing collateral, but it is still going to be a difficult process.

Also, keep in mind that if you fail to pay back a business loan, you will also lose whatever you used as underlying collateral.

## GOVERNMENT GRANTS AND LOANS

There are often special grant and/or loan programs offered by the federal, state and/or local government through traditional lenders or non-profit intermediaries to help start-up a new business. Many of these programs target a specific type of industry, certain types of business owners, a designated geographic location or a specific amount of funding.

## PEER-TO-PEER LENDING SITES

This is a relatively new option that has started to emerge in the last few years. These peer-to-peer (P2P) or social lending websites offer opportunities for businesses to get funding from individual and/or institutional investors. These sites allow you to apply for loans and investors can decide whether or not they want to fund your business.

Once you have found a source of funds and raised the necessary capital, there are a couple of other important steps to take. First, let's consider why it is important that you choose a fiscal year for your LLC and how you do his.

# CHOOSING A FISCAL YEAR

In order to determine the fiscal year for your LLC, you will need to check your datebook and have some basic accounting skills. As with any business, it is key to keep consistent records of your yearly revenues and expenses within an annual accounting period.

When keeping your accounting books, the IRS recognizes two types of taxable or tax years: 1) a calendar tax year and 2) a fiscal tax year. The structure and cycle of your business will help determine which of these two is appropriate for you. Let's first look at the definition of these two options.

## CALENDAR TAX YEAR

The calendar year is twelve consecutive months from January 1st to December 31st. Most small businesses choose to use the calendar year as the preferred tax year.

# Fiscal Tax Year

A fiscal tax year is twelve consecutive months that end on the final day of any month other than December. A fiscal tax year can also be a 52 to 53 week tax year that doesn't end on the last day of a month. With a fiscal year, your tax year always ends on the same day of the week when it lasts occurs in the calendar month. For example, the last Wednesday in March. It can also fall on the nearest to the last day of the month.

The LLC is created under state law, and owners are known as members. The federal government doesn't recognize the LLC as an official business classification when it comes to income tax purposes. Rather LLCs are taxed either as a sole proprietor, partnership or corporation when it comes to federal income tax.

You can sometimes choose how your LLC will be classified in an IRS filing. Often the state income tax authorities will follow IRS classifications when it comes to LLCs. To determine which classification and tax year make the most sense for your LLC you should talk with an accountant or tax professional. But let's take a moment to look at each of your options.

## Single Member LLC

This is for an LLC that has only one owner. This option is like a sole proprietor in that the single member LLC files individual income tax returns and uses a calendar year. This option is simple and easy to track.

## Partnership

LLCs that have two or more members may want to consider filing as a partnership. When you file as a partnership the taxable year applies to all members' tax years. If the members are currently paying income taxes based on a calendar year, then the LLC will do the same. If each member has a different tax year, then IRS guidelines will look for other determining factors such as the tax year for the LLC members that have a majority interest or the principal members or a tax year that yields the least combined deferral of partner income.

## Corporation

For LLC with one or more members, you can also choose to be classified as an S corporation or a C corporation. Owners of an S corporation typically use a calendar year, but some situation may get a different tax year after approval from the IRS. A C corporation files separate corporate income tax from the individual owners and offer the most flexibility to choose a calendar or fiscal year.

Once you've established your taxable year, you need to follow it in all subsequent years, and it can be very difficult to change. However, you can change it if you have a valid business reason, such as adjusting for a seasonal or cyclical business. In order to change your tax year, you must place a formal request to the IRS and receive approval in advance. The IRS tries to avoid such situations since they can result in a lost or distortion of revenues.

When it comes to taxes, consider the following forms and publications to help you make your decisions. Plus keep reading this guide as we'll have more specifics on taxes soon.

- LLC Taxation - Publication 3402, Taxation of Limited Liability Companies
- Calendar and Fiscal Tax Years - Publication 583, Starting a Business and Keeping Records
- Elect LLC Business Classification - Form 8832, Entity Classification Election

- Electing a Different Tax Year - Form 8716, Election to Have a Tax Year Other Than a Required Tax Year
- Request Change to Tax Year - Form 1128, Application to Adopt, Change, or Retain a Tax Year

## EIN FROM IRS

My advice is, once you file an LLC, you can seek help from an accountant or a CPA to file the appropriate IRS form on your behalf along with filling for an EIN (Employer's Identification Number). This number is similar to your social security number for it is for your business. It is a unique nine digit number that IRS assigns each business.

Remember you will not need this number if you choose to be a sole proprietorship for your business.

It is simple to apply, either you can do it yourself or get your accountant to apply for you, but the process is simple, you fill out the form SS-4, which can be filed online, via Fax or via mail. Once filed online you can receive the number is just a few hours.

Here is a link to IRS website where you can download or fill out the form online.

https://www.irs.gov/businesses/small-businesses-self-employed/how-to-apply-for-an-ein

Another important financial arrangement you need when starting an LLC is to open a business bank account. Let's briefly look at this important step.

# Opening a Business Bank Account

A basic task for any small business startup is to open a business bank account. There are several reasons why it is a good idea to have a separate bank account for your business. Establishing a business bank account is easy and quick with just a few necessary documents. Let's consider this vital step in starting your LLC.

## Why Get a Business Bank Account

There are several reasons why it is a good idea to open a separate business bank account.

First, having a separate bank account makes it easier to keep business expenses separate from personal expenses. It will also make it easier to work with an account should you choose to hire one.

Second, when you start an LLC, a separate bank account is often necessary since your business is legally distinct from the individual members. Having a separate business bank account allows you to keep your business accounts separate from personal accounts.

Third, having a separate business bank account makes it easier for you to manage and pay taxes for your business. Including paying estimated quarterly taxes.

Lastly, when you have a separate business bank account, it makes your company appear more professional and real instead of small and potentially unstable operation.

## Documents You Will Need

The necessary documents for setting up a business bank account is going to depend on how you organized your business. For example, a sole proprietor operation is going to require different documents from an LLC. Let's look at what papers you are going to need to start a separate business bank account for your LLC.

An LLC is going to need the company's EIN and a copy for the articles of organization or other equivalent document. If you don't have enough information in your articles of organization to show who is authorized to sign on behalf of the LLC, then you'll also need a document that provides this information.

## Opening An Account

Once you have the appropriate documents, you need to choose what type of bank account you want to open. You will have a range of options including a basic checking account that can have no monthly fees up to a more expansive account that offers additional features such as cash management services and other special services. No matter what type of account you choose, you will likely also want to get a debit card for your business. This will make it easier to pay for certain business expenses.

Often you can open your business bank account online without having to go in person to a bank. However, there are some types of businesses that won't be able to open their accounts online. This includes business that provides money services such as check cashing, issuing money orders, exchanging currency and wiring funds. It also applies to telemarketing business, those that deal in precious metals, gambling businesses and government entities.

If you are changing your business from a different form to an LLC, such as changing from a corporation to an LLC, then you'll want to open a new bank account for the business in its new form. To do this, you should have a new taxpayer ID number for the new business, which you will present to the bank along with the articles of incorporation and any other required documents.

## TYPES OF COMMERCIAL ACCOUNTS

Remember to read and understand various types of commercial checking account fees; you want to find a bank that offers free or almost free commercial checking account because some larger banks can charge you hundreds of dollars each month depending on how many transactions you do. Make sure to ask and shop around before you sign on the dotted line.

## OTHER KEY FACTORS

Once you have a separate bank account established for your LLC you want to manage it responsibly. Do this by maintaining an adequate balance, avoid writing bad checks and sticking with the same bank. This can help to increase your chances of getting a business loan from your bank if needed.

The last thing you need to consider before starting your LLC is the crucial step in establishing a registered agent.

# Registered Agent

The registered agent for an LLC is an individual who is designated to receive official papers on behalf of the business. This includes documents related to lawsuits and other important communications from the state such as renewal notices. A registered agent is needed in any state where you are registered to do business. The agent is "registered" in the sense that you submit a form to the state that the individual is the businesses agent for all official communications.

If you are just starting your LLC, you will need to designate your initial registered agent in your articles of incorporation. If you have already registered your business in a state, then you can often find a form through the Secretary of State that allows you to update your information with the state.

A registered agent needs to be located in the same state as the business. In addition to providing a name, you also need to provide a physical street address. This ensures that all documents can be served personally at an actual, physical address in accordance with statutory rules.

Often the registered agent is you or another member of the LLC such as a partner or a member. Often for a small business, the address for the registered agent is the same as the business location. You can choose to appoint a separate individual like a lawyer to act as a registered agent for your LLC. Occasionally you may choose to rely on a registered-agent company.

After you have everything ready, you can start running your LLC. Before we get into the state by state guide for starting your LLC, let's briefly look at some important things you need to know about running an LLC.

# RUNNING AN LLC

Just because you've successfully started up your LLC doesn't mean the hard work is done. Once you have a functioning LLC, there are still a lot of things you need to do on an annual basis in order to keep your business running legally. Let's take a look at these areas and then we'll include specifics at the end of this book in the state by state guide.

## RECORD KEEPING RULES

As we already discussed an LLC is a popular choice for many new businesses since they get the protection of a corporation, but avoid many of the record keeping issues of other business structures. While the levels of record keeping are less for LLCs, there are still recordkeeping rules you need to follow in order for your LLC to maintain its limited liability status.

The documents you need to keep for your LLC will vary based on your states' laws. However, at a minimum, you should keep records that are related to your companies' finances and organization.

## DOCUMENTS OF ORGANIZATION

This area includes the formation documentation that you filed with the Secretary of State's Office. In most states, this is known as the articles of organization. At a minimum, these documents contain your LLC's name, its purpose, its address and the name and address of the registered agent.

You should also keep a copy of any amendments you make to these articles. In addition, you want to keep a copy of any certificates or other documents that you receive from the secretary of state's office that recognize the creation of your LLC.

You should also keep a copy of your LLC's operating agreement and any amendments made to it. These copies should be kept at your business's principal office location. The operating agreement typically includes the following:

- ☐ The capital contribution of each member and any agreement to future contributions.
- ☐ How profits and losses are distributed among members.
- ☐ Members' rights to receive distributions.
- ☐ Member's voting rights.

- Procedures for member withdrawal and member admittance.
- Events that can lead to the dissolution of the LLC.

If you have any of this above information in a different document besides the operating agreement, then you should keep a copy of that document in the official records as well.

Your records should also contain an up-to-date list that is maintained with the full names and addresses of all current and past members. You should also include a list of all current and past managers along with their full names and addresses.

While state laws do not require LLCs to hold meetings, you can choose to require meetings by placing a meeting requirement provision in your operating agreement. We'll discuss this more shortly. In the meanwhile, if your LLC holds a meeting whether required or not then it is best to keep an accurate record of the meeting minutes including the following:

- The attendance record of the members.
- Any decisions made or votes cast.

- ☐ Any other information that is viewed as helpful to contain in an official record.

## FINANCIAL AND TAX DOCUMENTS

It is important that you keep your income tax returns. Any federal, state and local income tax returns need to be maintained for a minimum of three years, which is the time frame for which the IRS can audit your business. However, if fraud is suspected, there is no statute of limitations so you should permanently keep all tax records for best practice.

It is also a good idea to retain records supporting all expenses, credits, and income that your business reports. These records should be maintained for at least three years and should include the following:

- Deposit slips for your business bank account.
- Credit card statements for the business.
- Invoices.
- Canceled checks.
- Paid bills.

If your LLC has employees, you need to pay employment taxes, and you need to keep records on these. The IRS recommends that you retain all employment tax records for at least four years. You should keep the following in relation to your employment tax records:

- Employee information including name, address, Social Security number and dates of employment.
- Dates and all payments made to employees.
- Time slips or other records.
- W-4 forms.
- Copies of employment tax returns.

Lastly, an LLC should keep financial statements for a minimum of three years. This includes any important financial records or business contracts.

These are the records you need to keep, but you also need to know about filing annual reports, holding meetings and tax requirements. So let's move on to the important annual reports that you'll have to file.

# ANNUAL REPORTS

If you are the owner or member of an LLC, then you should become familiar with the annual report filing requirement for your state. The annual report for an LLC is sometimes known as a "Statement of Information." Whatever the name, they are filed with the appropriate state administrative agency or regulatory authority.

Each state has different rules on whether you need to file an annual report, how often you need to file and when to file, the amount of filing fees to be paid and what documents need to be filed if there are any changes to the LLC. When putting together your Statement of Information, you should consider the following.

The first thing you need to determine is whether or not you need to file an LLC annual report. Most states are trying to improve their business climate, so they don't require LLCs to make and file annual reports. However, some states do require an annual report. These reports allow the government state authority to determine the state of the LLC and ensure it is still operating. Most states provide you with a simple form that you need to fill out and typically ask for information such as the LLC's name and federal identification number, principal place of business and the purpose of the business, the identity, and addresses of the owners, authorized signatures for legal documents and registered agents for serving regulatory or court documents.

In some states, you may need to fill out other government forms if you are going to make material changes like amending your name or voluntarily dissolving the LLC.

The next thing you need to determine is how often you need to file your annual reports. In some states, the term "annual" report is a misnomer since not all states require the filing of a yearly Statement of Information. The time period between your reports often varies depending on the laws in the state where you do business. In some states, after your initial filing, you need to file biennially or every other year. For example, in Pennsylvania, you are only required to file reports every ten years.

Next, you need to determine the filing dates for your annual reports. In addition to knowing how often you need to file, you also want to determine the appropriate date or deadline for filing. States often determine their own deadlines for filing. Some states have a set uniform date for all LLCs to file. Other states have LLCs file on or before their anniversary date of filing the formation documents. Still, other states have a range of several months in which to file your report.

It is also important that you determine the cost of filing your annual report. Depending on your state, you may need to pay a fee to file your Statement of Information. The fee will vary greatly depending on your state, and you may need to set aside these funds in advance.

You should also learn about the consequences of failing to file your annual reports. There are a range of potential consequences that can occur if you fail to file your Statement of Information. In some states, the authority can involuntarily or administratively dissolve your business if you don't file on time.

In other states, you may need to pay outstanding fees or taxes plus late penalties if you want to maintain your LLC status. If you lose your status as an LLC, then you'll lose your limited liability protections. You could also end up breaching or defaulting on your duties in the operating agreement or your loan and insurance obligations.

It is good that most states keep LLC report to a minimum and often allow you to report online so there are minimal paperwork and mailing costs. Check with your Secretary of State's Office or other relevant agency to determine your current requirements. There will also be this information at the end of this guide.

As we discussed earlier, meetings aren't required of an LLC; but they can be a good idea. Let's consider meetings and why they are a good idea for your business.

## MEETINGS

The most basic advantage of having a formal business entity for entrepreneurs is being able to have liability protection. As a business owner, you would likely prefer to focus on the aspects of running your business rather than focusing on the formalities of the business.

However, there are some formalities that are important to help shield you from liability. Often the corporation was a way for business owners to limit their liability. The main disadvantage of a corporation is that the limited liability shield is lost if the owners don't follow strict formalities such as holding meetings. The LLC business model is very popular since it doesn't have the same strict corporate formalities while still offering the benefits of limited liability.

Holding meetings isn't a requirement of owning an LLC, but it is an important part. If you don't hold meetings, you won't lose your liability protection. So why should you consider doing them. Let's look at the requirements and why you should consider holding meetings for your LLC.

## MEETING REQUIREMENTS

While there are no specific requirements for an LLC to hold meetings, it may be placed as a requirement in the LLC organizational documents. The organizational documents of the LLC often include the articles of organization or a certificate of formation and an operating agreement.

If you fail to hold meetings, it often won't result in a loss of liability protection unless there is a requirement listed in one of these documents. If it is in one of these documents, then you'll need to comply with the provisions. However, the LLC owners can always amend the organizational document if meetings are deemed something the business doesn't need.

## Member Consent in Place of Meetings

If organizational documents contain a requirement for meetings, there is an alternative to help meet this requirement. This alternative is a written unanimous consent in place of a meeting. Rather than holding a meeting, the owners or members of the LLC can draft a document detailing the actions to be taken on behalf of the company.

This document must be signed by each member in order to satisfy the meeting requirements since it becomes a substitute for holding a meeting.

## Why Hold Meetings

Even though there are no requirements for an LLC to hold meetings, there are still plenty of reasons why you should hold meetings and keep accurate recordings of them.

One reason is to encourage discussions among members before making any major decisions such as electing managers, issuing dividends and admitting new members. Another reason is to keep all your members informed and up-to-date on the actions of the LLC.

Perhaps the most important reason is, so you have accurate records and evidence that the LLC is following company formalities. Should any dispute arise among members, it will provide a clear record of discussions, votes, and actions taken by the company.

The last thing I need to discuss before moving on the state by state guide is to discuss how your LLC is taxed and what documents you need to file for this.

## How LLCs Are Taxed

An LLC isn't a separate tax entity like a corporation. Rather the IRS considers it a "pass-through entity" similar to a partnership or sole proprietorship. This means that all the profits and losses of the business "pass through" to the owner or members, who report it on their personal tax returns. The business itself doesn't pay federal income taxes, but some states do require the business to pay annual taxes.

### Income Taxes

Whether the IRS treats your business as a partnership or a sole proprietorship will depend on the number of members you have.

## SINGLE-OWNER/MEMBER LLCS

For tax purposes, the IRS treats LLCs as a sole proprietorship. This means the business doesn't pay taxes and doesn't need to file a return with the IRS. As the sole owner, you are required to report all profits or losses on Schedule C and submit a 1040 tax return.

## MULTI-OWNER/MEMBER LLCS

A co-owned LLC is viewed as a partnership for tax purposes with the IRS. These business also don't pay taxes on business income. The LLC owners each pay taxes on their share of the profits through their own personal income tax returns. In this situation, it is important to have each member's distributive share of profits and losses set out in the operating agreement.

## IRS FORM 1065

Even though an LLC doesn't pay its own income taxes, it still needs to file Form 1065 with the IRS. This is an informal return that the IRS reviews in order to make sure the members are reporting their income correctly. Each member of the LLC is provided with a Schedule K-1 to break down each members shares. The members then report the profits and losses on their own Form 1040 with a Schedule E attachment.

## ELECTING CORPORATE TAXATION

If you have a business that needs to maintain a high amount of profits known as retained earnings; then you might want to consider electing corporate taxation. This is when the LLC can choose to be treated like a corporation for tax purposes only. This is done by filing IRS Form 8832, Entity Classification Election. Be sure to check the corporate tax treatment box.

As of 2018, all regular corporations are taxed at a flat rate of 21% on all profits. This rate is less than the top three individual income tax rates that range from 32% to 37%, which would apply to LLC members based on their income levels. When choosing to be taxed as a corporation, LLC members can save on their overall taxes.

However, it isn't all the benefits. The savings can be elusive since money distributed from a corporation to the owners faced double taxation. First, the 21% corporate tax needs to be paid, and then the shareholders pay individual income tax on their dividends at the capital gains rates, which can be up to 23.8%.

The benefit is that retained earnings aren't double taxed. By choosing to elect corporate taxation, LLC can offer other tax-advantaged benefits to owners and employees such as stock options and stock ownership plans; none of them face double taxation.

## ESTIMATING AND PAYING INCOME TAXES

Members of an LLC are viewed as self-employed business owners rather than employees, so they aren't subject to tax withholding. Rather each member is responsible for setting enough money aside to pay taxes on their share of profits. Members need to estimate the amount of tax they'll owe for a year and make quarterly payments to the IRS in April, June, September, and January.

## SELF-EMPLOYMENT TAXES

Since members of an LLC aren't employees, there is no withholding of Social Security and Medicare contributions from their paychecks. Rather, most LLC owners are required to pay these taxes known as "self-employment taxes" directly to the IRS.

Any owner who works in or helps manage the LLC must pay this tax on their distributive share. The owner who is not active in the LLC is exempt from paying self-employment taxes on their profit shares. This area of regulations is a bit complicated, but if you actively work in your LLC, then you can expect to pay self-employment tax on any profits you receive.

Those who are subject to the self-employment tax needs to report the amount due on Schedule SE and submit it annually with the tax return. LLC owners will pay twice as much self-employment tax as regular employees since an employee's contributions to this tax are matched by employers.

On the other hand, LLC owners can also deduct half of their taxable income which saves a little bit of money. For business owners, the self-employment tax rate is 15.3% of net income up to an annual threshold and then 2.9% for everything above that. The IRS website publishes these annual threshold amounts.

## DEDUCTIONS AND EXPENSES

Most of the money your business spends on either income taxes or self-employment taxes doesn't have to pay additional taxes. You can deduct legitimate business expenses from your income, which can reduce the number of profits you have to report to the IRS. Some common deductible expenses include start-up costs, automobile and travel expenses, equipment costs and advertising and/or promotion costs.

LLC owners can also be eligible for a new income tax deduction that was established by the Tax Cuts and Jobs Act. This started in 2018 and allows LLC owners to deduct for income tax purposes up to 20% of the net income from the entity. However, if the taxable income goes beyond the annual threshold, then the deduction is limited to 50% of the amount paid to employees of the entity.

The deduction is also phased out for taxpayers that are involved in different service businesses. This deduction is also not available to LLCs that choose to be taxed as corporations.

## STATE FEES AND TAXES

Most states tax profits from an LLC the same way the IRS does. The LLC owners will pay taxes to the state based on their personal returns, while the business itself doesn't pay any state taxes.

In some states, you are required to pay additional taxes. These taxes are based on the amount of income the LLC makes in addition to the income tax that the owners pay.

Some state also requires annual fees. These fees aren't income-related. These are known as "franchise tax," "annual registration fee" or a "renewal fee." This fee is often about $100 but can be as high as $800. Before forming an LLC, it is a good idea to determine whether or not your state charges a separate tax or fee.

Now that we know everything we need about forming an LLC let's look at individual requirements based on the states.

# PART -2

# STATE BY STATE GUIDE TO FORMING AN LLC

# ALABAMA

1. Name Reservation

    Name Search:

    http://arc-sos.state.al.us/CGI/CORPNAME.MBR/INPUT

    Must end with one of three designators:
    - ☐ LLC
    - ☐ L.L.C.
    - ☐ Limited Liability Company

    Reserved with: Alabama Secretary of State

    Cost: $10 by mail and $28 online

    To File:

    https://www.alabamainteractive.org/sos/introduction_input.action

2. Registered Agent

    Required in the state of Alabama

3. Filing Forms and Fees
    - $183
    - Form SOSDF-8:

    http://sos.alabama.gov/sites/default/files/2017-03/sosdf-8.pdf
    - Filed with the Probate Judge by mail

4. Operating Agreement and Publishing Requirements

   Not required, but advised

   No publishing requirements

5. Tax ID Number (EIN)

   Through the IRS online or by mail with Form SS-4: https://sa.www4.irs.gov/modiein/individual/index.jsp

6. Annual Requirements and Taxes
   - Must file an Annual Report and a Business Privilege Tax Return with the Alabama Department of Revenue.
   - Must file the Initial Business Privilege Tax Return within 2 months and 2 weeks of formation.
   - Due by April 15th of each year.
   - $100 minimum
   - https://revenue.alabama.gov/forms/

7. Licenses and Permits
   - A Business Privilege License is required for your county.
   - A Store License is needed to buy and sell physical goods.
   - Issued through the County Probate Office or County Licensing Commission

# ALASKA

1. Name Reservation

    Name Search:

    https://www.commerce.alaska.gov/cbp/main/search/entities

    Must end with one of the following designations:
    - LLC
    - L.L.C.
    - Ltd. Liability Co.
    - Ltd. Liability Company
    - Limited Liability Co.
    - Limited Liability Company

    Cannot include a designator that makes it sound like another business entity.

    Can include the name of a city, village or borough; but not the words themselves.

2. Registered Agent

    Required in the state of Alaska

3. Filing Forms and Fees
    - $250
    - Form 08-484:

        https://www.commerce.alaska.gov/

CBP/Corporation/startpage.aspx?file=CRFIL&entity=LLCO&isforeign=N
- Filed with the State of Alaska, Corporations Section

4. Operating Agreement and Publishing Requirements

    Needed when opening a bank account

    No publishing requirements

5. Tax ID Number (EIN)

    Through the IRS online or by mail with Form SS-4: https://sa.www4.irs.gov/modiein/individual/index.jsp

6. Annual Requirements and Taxes
    - Must file an Initial Report within 6 months of formation.
    - Biennial Report due every 2 years by January 2nd.
    - Initial Report online: https://www.commerce.alaska.gov/CBP/Corporation/startpage.aspx?file=IBRPT
    - $100
    - Biennial Report online: https://www.commerce.alaska.gov/

CBP/Corporation/startpage.aspx?file=BIRPT

7. Licenses and Permits
    - Must have a general business license:
        - $50
        - Renewed yearly
        - https://www.commerce.alaska.gov/cbp/businesslicensing/New.aspx#

# ARIZONA

1. Name Reservation

    Name Search:

    http://ecorp.azcc.gov/Search

    Must end with one of two designations:
    - ☐ LLC
    - ☐ L.L.C.

2. Registered Agent

    Required in the state of Arizona and known as a Statutory Agent

3. Filing Forms and Fees
    - $50
    - Form L010:

        http://www.azcc.gov/Divisions/Corporations/forms/starpas/formsSTPS/L010-Articles-of-Organization.pdf?d=153
    - Also need a Cover Sheet, Statutory Agent Acceptance and Membership Attachment
    - Filed with Arizona Corporation Commission

        http://ecorp.azcc.gov/efiling

4. Operating Agreement and Publishing Requirements

    Not required in Arizona but recommended.

Must publish Articles in a general circulation newspaper in the county of business

within 60 days for 3 consecutive publications.

5. Tax ID Number (EIN)

Through the IRS online or by mail with Form SS-4: https://sa.www4.irs.gov/modiein/individual/index.jsp

6. Annual Requirements and Taxes

No annual filing required

If you are collecting sales tax or employing people, then you'll need to apply with

the Arizona Department of Revenue.

7. Licenses and Permits

Vary depending on the parts of the state you are doing business in and what type

of business, you are doing.

# ARKANSAS

1. Name Reservation

    Name Search:

    http://www.sos.arkansas.gov/corps/search_all.php

    Must end with one of two designations:
    - ☐ LLC
    - ☐ L.L.C.

2. Registered Agent

    Required in the state of Arkansas

3. Filing Forms and Fees
    - $50
    - Form LL-01:

    https://www.sos.arkansas.gov/uploads/bcs/LL-01.pdf

    - Filed with Arkansas Secretary of State
    - File online:

        https://www.ark.org/sos/ofs/docs/index.php

4. Operating Agreement and Publishing Requirements

Not required in the state of Arkansas, but recommended.

No publishing requirements.

5. Tax ID Number (EIN)

Through the IRS online or by mail with Form SS-4: https://sa.www4.irs.gov/modiein/individual/index.jsp

6. Annual Requirements and Taxes
   - Must file Annual Reports
   - Due on May 1st of every year, unless it is a Sunday
   - $150
   - Filed with Arkansas Secretary of State
   - https://www.sos.arkansas.gov/business-commercial-services-bcs/franchise-tax/franchise-tax-report-forms

7. Licenses and Permits

Depends on the parts of the state you are doing business in and what business you are doing.

# CALIFORNIA

1. Name Reservation

    Name Search:

    https://businesssearch.sos.ca.gov/

    Must end with one of the following designators:
    - ☐ LLC
    - ☐ L.L.C.
    - ☐ Limited Liability Company
    - ☐ Limited Liability Co.
    - ☐ Ltd. Liability Company
    - ☐ Ltd. Liability Co.

2. Registered Agent

    Required in the state of California

3. Filing Forms and Fees
    - $70
    - Form LLC-1:

        http://bpd.cdn.sos.ca.gov/llc/forms/llc-1.pdf

    - Filed with California Secretary of State

4. Operating Agreement and Publishing Requirements

    Not required but recommended

    No publishing requirements

5. Tax ID Number (EIN)

Through the IRS online or by mail with Form SS-4: https://sa.www4.irs.gov/modiein/individual/index.jsp

6. Annual Requirements and Taxes
   - Must file an Initial Statement of Information within 90 days of formation.
   - Form LLC-12: https://llcbizfile.sos.ca.gov/
   - Costs: $20
   - Filed with California Secretary of State
   - Ongoing Statement of Information filed every 2 years.
   - Due by the anniversary date of approval.
7. Licenses and Permits
   - Must pay $800 Franchise Tax each year.
   - Paid to California Franchise Tax Board
   - Form 3522:

   https://www.ftb.ca.gov/forms/search/index.aspx
   - Additional permits and licenses will vary depending on where you do business and what type of business you do.

# COLORADO

1. Name Reservation

   Name Search:

   http://www.sos.state.co.us/biz/BusinessEntityCriteriaExt.do

2. Registered Agent

   Required in the state of Colorado

3. Filing Forms and Fees
   - $50
   - http://www.sos.state.co.us/biz/FileDoc.do
   - Must file an Additional Members form if you have more than 2 members.
   - Filed with Colorado Secretary of State

4. Operating Agreement and Publishing Requirements

   No required but recommended.

   No publishing requirements.

5. Tax ID Number (EIN)

   Through the IRS online or by mail with Form SS-4: https://sa.www4.irs.gov/modiein/individual/index.jsp

6. Annual Requirements and Taxes

- Filed with Secretary of State
- http://www.sos.state.co.us/biz/FileDocSearchCriteria.do
- Costs: $10
- Filed in the month you formed your LLC, but allowed to file in the two months before or after your formation month.

7. Licenses and Permits
   - Varies depending on where your business is located and what type of business you are doing.

# CONNECTICUT

1. Name Reservation

    Name Search:

    http://www.concord-sots.ct.gov/CONCORD/online?sn=PublicInquiry&eid=9740

    Must have one of the following designators:
    - ☐ LLC
    - ☐ L.L.C.

    Cannot contain any of the following designators:
    - ☐ Corporation
    - ☐ Incorporated
    - ☐ Corp.
    - ☐ Inc.

2. Registered Agent

    Required in the state of Connecticut

3. Filing Forms and Fees
    - $160
    - https://www.concord-sots.ct.gov/CONCORD/customer?eid=4703
    - Filed with Secretary of State

4. Operating Agreement and Publishing Requirements

   No required but recommended.

   No publishing requirements.

5. Tax ID Number (EIN)

   Through the IRS online or by mail with Form SS-4: https://sa.www4.irs.gov/modiein/individual/index.jsp

6. Annual Requirements and Taxes
   - Required to file an annual report each year.
   - Costs: $20
   - Due every year by the end of your anniversary month.
   - http://www.concord-sots.ct.gov/CONCORD/index.jsp
   - Filed with Connecticut Secretary of State

7. Licenses and Permits

   Varies depending on where you are and what type of business you do.

# DELAWARE

1. Name Reservation

    Name Search:

    https://icis.corp.delaware.gov/Ecorp/NameReserv/NameReservation.aspx

    **Must contain one of the following designators:**
    - ☐ LLC
    - ☐ L.L.C.

    Cannot contain any of the following designators:
    - ☐ Corporation
    - ☐ Incorporated
    - ☐ Corp.
    - ☐ Inc.

2. Registered Agent

    Required in the state of Delaware.

3. Filing Forms and Fees
    - $90
    - http://corp.delaware.gov/llcform09.pdf
    - Filed with Delaware Division of Corporations

4. Operating Agreement and Publishing Requirements

    Not required, but recommended.

    No publishing requirements.

5. Tax ID Number (EIN)

Through the IRS online or by mail with Form SS-4: https://sa.www4.irs.gov/modiein/individual/index.jsp

6. Annual Requirements and Taxes
   - No Annual Report required.
   - Must pay $300 Annual Franchise Tax.
   - Due by June 1st of each year.
   - Filed online: https://icis.corp.delaware.gov/Ecorp/logintax.aspx?FilingType=FranchiseTax
   - Filed with Delaware Secretary of State.

7. Licenses and Permits

Varies depending on business location and type of business you do.

# DISTRICT OF COLUMBIA

1. Name Reservation

    Name Search:

    https://corp.dcra.dc.gov/Account.aspx/LogOn?ReturnUrl=%2f

    Must end with one of the following designators:
    - ☐ LLC
    - ☐ Limited Liability Company

2. Registered Agent

    Required in the District of Columbia

3. Filing Forms and Fees
    - $220
    - Form DLC-1
    - Filed with the Corporations Division

4. Operating Agreement and Publishing Requirements

    Not required, but recommended.

    No publishing requirements.

5. Tax ID Number (EIN)

    Through the IRS online or by mail with Form SS-4:

    https://sa.www4.irs.gov/modiein/individual/index.jsp

6. Annual Requirements and Taxes
    - Biannual reports required

- Filed with the Department of Consumer and Regulatory Affairs
- Costs $300
- Form BRA-25
- Due by April 1st of each following year

7. Licenses and Permits

Varies based on location and type of business.

# FLORIDA

1. Name Reservation

    Name Search:

    http://search.sunbiz.org/Inquiry/CorporationSearch/ByName

    Must contain one of the following designators:
    - ☐ LLC
    - ☐ L.L.C.
    - ☐ Limited Liability Company

2. Registered Agent

    Required in the state of Florida.

3. Filing Forms and Fees
    - $125
    - Form CR2E047:

        https://efile.sunbiz.org/llc_file.html
    - Filed with the Department of State

4. Operating Agreement and Publishing Requirements

    Not required, but recommended.

    No publishing requirements.

5. Tax ID Number (EIN)

    Through the IRS online or by mail with Form SS-4:

    https://sa.www4.irs.gov/modiein/individual/index.jsp

6. Annual Requirements and Taxes
    - Must file an Annual Report each year.
    - Costs: $138.75
    - Due by May 1st of each year.
    - Filed with the Department of State
    - https://services.sunbiz.org/Filings/AnnualReport/FilingStart
7. Licenses and Permits

Varies depending on your location and type of business.

# GEORGIA

1. Name Reservation

    Name Search:

    https://ecorp.sos.ga.gov/BusinessSearch

    Must end with one of the following designators:

    - ☐ LLC
    - ☐ L.L.C.
    - ☐ Limited Liability Company
    - ☐ Limited Liability Co.
    - ☐ Ltd. Liability Company
    - ☐ Ltd. Liability Co.
    - ☐ LC
    - ☐ L.C.

2. Registered Agent

    Required in the state of Georgia.

3. Filing Forms and Fees
    - $100
    - Form CD 030 and 231:

        https://ecorp.sos.ga.gov/
    - Filed with Corporations Division

4. Operating Agreement and Publishing Requirements

    Not required, but recommended.

    No publishing requirements.

5. Tax ID Number (EIN)

    Through the IRS online or by mail with Form SS-4: https://sa.www4.irs.gov/modiein/individual/index.jsp

6. Annual Requirements and Taxes
    - Must file an Annual Report each year.
    - Due between January 1st and April 1st of each year.
    - Costs: $50
    - https://ecorp.sos.ga.gov/

7. Licenses and Permits

    Depends on where your business is and what type of business you do.

# HAWAII

1. Name Reservation

    Name Search:

    https://hbe.ehawaii.gov/documents/search.html

    Must end in one of the following designators:
    - LLC
    - L.L.C.

    Cannot end with one of the following designators:
    - Corporation
    - Incorporated
    - Corp.
    - Inc.

2. Registered Agent

    Required in the state of Hawaii

3. Filing Forms and Fees
    - $50
    - Form LLC-1:

    http://files.hawaii.gov/dcca/breg/registration/forms/llc-1.pdf
    - Filed with Business Registration Division

- File online:

    https://hbe.ehawaii.gov/BizEx/home.eb

4. Operating Agreement and Publishing Requirements

    Not required, but recommended.

    No publishing requirements.

5. Tax ID Number (EIN)

    Through the IRS online or by mail with Form SS-4: https://sa.www4.irs.gov/modiein/individual/index.jsp

6. Annual Requirements and Taxes
    - Annual Report required each year.
    - Costs: $15
    - Annual Report Form:

    http://files.hawaii.gov/dcca/breg/registration/forms/c5.pdf

    - File online:

        https://hbe.ehawaii.gov/annuals/
    - Due date varies by LLC approval date.

7. Licenses and Permits

    Varies depending on business location and type of business.

# IDAHO

1. Name Reservation

    Name Search:

    https://www.accessidaho.org/public/sos/corp/search.html

    Must end with one of the following designators:
    - ☐ LLC
    - ☐ L.L.C.

    Cannot end with any of the following designators:
    - ☐ Corporation
    - ☐ Incorporated
    - ☐ Corp.
    - ☐ Inc.

2. Registered Agent

    Required in the state of Idaho

3. Filing Forms and Fees
    - $100
    - http://www.sos.idaho.gov/corp/2015/LLC%20Cert%20org%202015%20FILL.pdf
    - Filed with Secretary of State

4. Operating Agreement and Publishing Requirements

    Not required, but recommended.

No publishing requirements.

5. Tax ID Number (EIN)

Through the IRS online or by mail with Form SS-4:

https://sa.www4.irs.gov/modiein/individual/index.jsp

6. Annual Requirements and Taxes
    - Annual Report required each year.
    - No cost.
    - Do at the end of your anniversary month each year.
    - Annual Report Form:

http://www.sos.idaho.gov/CorpPrintForm/AnnualReport.html

    - Filed with Secretary of State
    - File online:
      http://www.sos.idaho.gov/corpar/Default.aspx

7. Licenses and Permits

Varies depending on where you do business and what type of business.

# ILLINOIS

1. Name Reservation

    Name Search:

    https://www.ilsos.gov/corporatellc/

    Must end with one of the following designators:

    - ☐ LLC
    - ☐ L.L.C.
    - ☐ Limited Liability Company

2. Registered Agent

    Required in the state of Illinois

3. Filing Forms and Fees
    - $150
    - Form LLC-5.5:

        http://www.cyberdriveillinois.com/publications/pdf_publications/llc55.pdf

    - Filed with Secretary of State
    - File online:

        https://www.ilsos.gov/llcarticles/index.jsp

4. Operating Agreement and Publishing Requirements

    No required but recommended.

    No publishing requirements.

5. Tax ID Number (EIN)

   Through the IRS online or by mail with Form SS-4: https://sa.www4.irs.gov/modiein/individual/index.jsp

6. Annual Requirements and Taxes
   - Required to file an Annual Report every year.
   - Due before the first of the month of your anniversary.
   - Costs: $75 by mail, $125 online.
   - Form LLC-50.1: http://www.cyberdriveillinois.com/publications/pdf_publications/llc501.pdf
   - Filed with Secretary of State
   - File online: https://www.ilsos.gov/llcarpt/

7. Licenses and Permits

   Varies depending on where your business is and what type of business you do.

# INDIANA

1. Name Reservation

   Name Search:

   https://bsd.sos.in.gov/publicbusinesssearch

   Must end with the following designators:
   - ☐ LLC
   - ☐ L.L.C.

   Must not end with the following designators:
   - ☐ Corporation
   - ☐ Incorporated
   - ☐ Corp.
   - ☐ Inc.

2. Registered Agent

   Required in the state of Indiana

3. Filing Forms and Fees
   - $90
   - Filed with Secretary of State

4. Operating Agreements and Publishing Requirements

   No required but recommended.

   No publishing requirements.

5. Tax ID Number (EIN)

   Through the IRS online or by mail with Form SS-4:

https://sa.www4.irs.gov/modiein/individual/index.jsp

6. Annual Requirements and Taxes
   - Required to file a Business Entity Report every 2 years.
   - Costs: $50 by mail, $31 online.
   - Due before the last day of the anniversary month.
   - Business Entity Form: http://www.in.gov/sos/business/2426.htm
   - Filed with Secretary of State.
7. Licenses and Permits

   Varies depending on location and type of business.

# IOWA

1. Name Reservation

    Name Search:

    https://sos.iowa.gov/search/business/search.aspx

    Must end with one of the following designators:
    - ☐ LLC
    - ☐ L.L.C.
    - ☐ Limited Liability Company
    - ☐ Limited Liability Co.
    - ☐ Ltd. Liability Company
    - ☐ Ltd. Liability Co.
    - ☐ LC
    - ☐ L.C.

2. Registered Agent

    Required in the state of Iowa

3. Filing Forms and Fees
    - $50
    - Filed with Secretary of State
    - File online:

        https://sos.iowa.gov/file/origination/index.aspx

4. Operating Agreements and Publishing Requirements

   No required but recommended.

   No publishing requirements.

5. Tax ID Number (EIN)

   Through the IRS online or by mail with Form SS-4: https://sa.www4.irs.gov/modiein/individual/index.jsp

6. Annual Requirements and Taxes
   - Required Biennial Report due every 2 years.
   - Due before January 1st and April 1st of odd number years.
   - Costs: $60 by mail, $45 online.
   - Biennial Report Form: https://sos.iowa.gov/file/br/login.aspx
   - Filed with Secretary of State.
   - File online: https://sos.iowa.gov/file/br/login.aspx

7. Licenses and Permits

   Varies depending on location and type of business.

# KANSAS

1. Name Reservation

   Name Search:

   https://www.kansas.gov/businesscenter/

   Must end in one of the following designators:
   - ☐ LLC
   - ☐ L.L.C.

   Cannot end with the following designators:
   - ☐ Corporation
   - ☐ Incorporated
   - ☐ Corp.
   - ☐ Inc.

2. Registered Agent

   Required in the state of Kansas

3. Filing Forms and Fees
   - $165
   - Form DL:

   https://www.sos.ks.gov/forms/business_services/DL.pdf
   - Filed with Secretary of State

4. Operating Agreements and Publishing Requirements

   Not required, but recommended.

No publishing requirements.

5. Tax ID Number (EIN)

    Through the IRS online or by mail with Form SS-4: https://sa.www4.irs.gov/modiein/individual/index.jsp

6. Annual Requirements and Taxes
    - Must file an Annual Report every year.
    - Costs $55
    - Due every year on the 15th day of the 4th month after tax closing month.
    - Form LC50:

    https://www.sos.ks.gov/forms/business_services/LC.pdf

    - Filed with Secretary of State
    - File online: https://www.kansas.gov/annual-reports/index.do

7. Licenses and Permits

    Varies depending on location and type of business.

# KENTUCKY

1. Name Reservation

    Name Search:

    https://app.sos.ky.gov/ftsearch/

    Must end with one of the following designators:

    - ☐ LLC
    - ☐ L.L.C.

    Cannot end with any of the following designators:

    - ☐ Corporation
    - ☐ Incorporated
    - ☐ Corp.
    - ☐ Inc.

2. Registered Agent

    Required in the state of Kentucky.

3. Filing Forms and Fees

    - $40
    - Form KLC:

        http://www.sos.ky.gov/bus/business-filings/Forms/Documents/AOProfit.PDF

    - Filed with Secretary of State

4. Operating Agreements and Publishing Requirements

Not required, but recommended.

No publishing requirements.

5. Tax ID Number (EIN)

    Through the IRS online or by mail with Form SS-4: https://sa.www4.irs.gov/modiein/individual/index.jsp

6. Annual Requirements and Taxes
    - Annual Report due every year.
    - Costs $15
    - Due between January 1st and June 30th each year.
    - Filed with Secretary of State.
    - File online: https://app.sos.ky.gov/ftsearch/?path=ftarp

7. Licenses and Permits

    Varies depending on location and type of business.

# LOUISIANA

1. Name Reservation

    Name Search:

    https://coraweb.sos.la.gov/CommercialSearch/CommercialSearch.aspx

    Must end in one of the following designators:
    - LLC
    - L.L.C.

    Cannot end in any of the following designators:
    - Corporation
    - Incorporated
    - Corp.
    - Inc.

2. Registered Agent

    Required in the state of Louisiana.

3. Filing Forms and Fees
    - $100
    - Form #365
    - Filed with Commercial Division

4. Operating Agreements and Publishing Requirements

    Not required, but recommended.

    No publishing requirements.

5. Tax ID Number (EIN)

Through the IRS online or by mail with Form SS-4: https://sa.www4.irs.gov/modiein/individual/index.jsp

6. Annual Requirements and Taxes
    - Must file an Annual Report each year.
    - Costs $35
    - Due before your anniversary date.
    - Filed with Commercial Division
7. Licenses and Permits

Varies based on location and type of business.

# MAINE

1. Name Reservation

   Name Search:

   https://icrs.informe.org/nei-sos-icrs/ICRS?MainPage=x

   Must end in one of the following designators:
   - ☐ LLC
   - ☐ L.L.C.

   Cannot end in any of the following designators:
   - ☐ Corporation
   - ☐ Incorporated
   - ☐ Corp.
   - ☐ Inc.

2. Registered Agent

   Required in the state of Maine.

3. Filing Forms and Fees
   - $175
   - Form MLLC-6:

   http://www.maine.gov/sos/cec/forms/mllc6.pdf

   - Filed with Secretary of State

4. Operating Agreements and Publishing Requirements

   No required but recommended.

   No publishing requirements.

5. Tax ID Number (EIN)

   Through the IRS online or by mail with Form SS-4: https://sa.www4.irs.gov/modiein/individual/index.jsp

6. Annual Requirements and Taxes
   - Annual Report required every year.
   - Costs $85
   - Due by June 1st of every year.
   - Annual Report Form: http://www10.informe.org/aro/form_download.html
   - Filed with Secretary of State
   - File online: https://www10.informe.org/aro/index_on.html

7. Licenses and Permits

   Varies by location and type of business.

# MARYLAND

1. Name Reservation

    Name Search:

    https://egov.maryland.gov/BusinessExpress/EntitySearch

    Must end in one of the following designators:
    - ☐ LLC
    - ☐ L.L.C.
    - ☐ Limited Liability Company
    - ☐ L.C.
    - ☐ LC

2. Registered Agent

    Required in the state of Maryland

3. Filing Forms and Fees
    - $100
    - Filed with Maryland Department of Assessments and Taxation
    - File online: https://egov.maryland.gov/BusinessExpress/

4. Operating Agreements and Publishing Requirements

    Not required, but recommended.

No publishing requirements.

5. Tax ID Number (EIN)

   Through the IRS online or by mail with Form SS-4: https://sa.www4.irs.gov/modiein/individual/index.jsp

6. Annual Requirements and Taxes
   - Annual Report required every year.
   - Due between January 1st and April 15th.
   - Costs $300 minimum.
   - Filed with the State of Maryland.
   - File online: https://egov.maryland.gov/businessexpress

7. Licenses and Permits

   Varies based on location and type of business.

# MASSACHUSETTS

1. Name Reservation

   Name Search:

   http://corp.sec.state.ma.us/corpweb/CorpSearch/CorpSearch.aspx

   Must end in one of the following designators:
   - ☐ LLC
   - ☐ L.L.C.

   Cannot end in any of the following designators:
   - ☐ Corporation
   - ☐ Incorporated
   - ☐ Corp.
   - ☐ Inc.

2. Registered Agent

   Required in the state of Massachusetts

3. Filing Forms and Fees
   - $500
   - Form D:

   http://www.sec.state.ma.us/cor/corpdf/c156c512dllccert.pdf
   - Filed with Secretary of the Commonwealth

- File online: https://corp.sec.state.ma.us/corp/loginsystem/login_form.asp?FilingMethod=I

4. Operating Agreements and Publishing Requirements

   Not required, but recommended.

   No publishing requirements.

5. Tax ID Number (EIN)

   Through the IRS online or by mail with Form SS-4: https://sa.www4.irs.gov/modiein/individual/index.jsp

6. Annual Requirements and Taxes
   - Annual Report must be filed every year.
   - Costs: $520
   - Due before the anniversary date.
   - Filed with Secretary of the Commonwealth.

7. Licenses and Permits

   Varies by the location and type of business.

# MICHIGAN

1. Name Reservation

   Name Search:

   https://cofs.lara.state.mi.us/corpweb/CorpSearch/CorpSearch.aspx

   Must end in one of the following designators:
   - ☐ LLC
   - ☐ L.L.C.
   - ☐ LC
   - ☐ L.C.
   - ☐ Limited Liability Company

   Cannot end in any of the following designators:
   - ☐ Corporation
   - ☐ Incorporated
   - ☐ Corp.
   - ☐ Inc.
   - ☐ Limited Partnership
   - ☐ LP
   - ☐ L.P.
   - ☐ Trust

2. Registered Agent

   Required in the state of Michigan.

3. Filing Forms and Fees
   - $50

- Form CSCL/CD-700
- Filed with Michigan Department of Licensing and Regulatory Affairs

4. Operating Agreements and Publishing Requirements

No required but recommended.

No publishing requirements.

5. Tax ID Number (EIN)

Through the IRS online or by mail with Form SS-4: https://sa.www4.irs.gov/modiein/individual/index.jsp

6. Annual Requirements and Taxes
   - Annual Statement must be filed every year.
   - Due by February 15th every year.
   - Costs $25
   - Filed with Michigan Department of Licensing and Regulatory Affairs

7. Licenses and Permits

Varies by location and type of business.

# MINNESOTA

1. Name Reservation

    Name Search:

    https://mblsportal.sos.state.mn.us/Business/Search

    Must end in one of the following designators:
    - ☐ LLC
    - ☐ L.L.C.

    Cannot end in any of the following designators:
    - ☐ Corporation
    - ☐ Incorporated
    - ☐ Corp.
    - ☐ Inc.

2. Registered Agent

    Required in the state of Minnesota

3. Filing Forms and Fees
    - $160
    - Form:

        http://www.sos.state.mn.us/media/1824/llcarticlesoforganization.pdf
    - Filed with MN Secretary of State - Business Services

4. Operating Agreements and Publishing Requirements

   No required but recommended.

   No publishing requirements.

5. Tax ID Number (EIN)

   Through the IRS online or by mail with Form SS-4: https://sa.www4.irs.gov/modiein/individual/index.jsp

6. Annual Requirements and Taxes
   - Must file an Annual Renewal each year.
   - No cost for business in good standing.
   - Due by December 31st of each year.
   - Form: http://www.sos.state.mn.us/media/1569/llcdomesticforeignrenewal.pdf
   - Filed with MN Secretary of State - Business Services

7. Licenses and Permits

   Varies based on location and type of business.

# MISSISSIPPI

1. Name Reservation

   Name Search:

   https://corp.sos.ms.gov/corp/portal/c/page/corpBusinessIdSearch/portal.aspx?#clear=1

   **Must end in one of the following designators:**
   - ☐ LLC
   - ☐ L.L.C.

   Cannot end in any of the following designators:
   - ☐ Corporation
   - ☐ Incorporation
   - ☐ Corp.
   - ☐ Inc.

2. Registered Agent

   Required in the state of Mississippi

3. Filing Forms and Fees
   - $50
   - Filed with Secretary of State

4. Operating Agreements and Publishing Requirements

   Not required, but recommended.

   No publishing requirements.

5. Tax ID Number (EIN)

   Through the IRS online or by mail with Form SS-4:

https://sa.www4.irs.gov/modiein/individual/index.jsp

6. Annual Requirements and Taxes
   - Must file an Annual Report every year.
   - No cost.
   - Due before April 15th of each year.
   - Filed with Secretary of State
7. Licenses and Permits

   Varies based on location and type of business.

# MISSOURI

1. Name Reservation

   Name Search:

   https://bsd.sos.mo.gov/BusinessEntity/BESearch.aspx

   Must end in one of the following designators:
   - LLC
   - L.L.C.

   Cannot end in any of the following designators:
   - Corporation
   - Incorporated
   - Corp.
   - Inc.

2. Registered Agent

   Required in the state of Missouri

3. Filing Forms and Fees
   - $105
   - Form LLC1:

   http://s1.sos.mo.gov/CMSImages/Business/llc1.pdf
   - Filed with Corporations Division

4. Operating Agreements and Publishing Requirements

   An operating agreement is required in the state of Missouri.

   No publishing requirements.

5. Tax ID Number (EIN)

   Through the IRS online or by mail with Form SS-4: https://sa.www4.irs.gov/modiein/individual/index.jsp

6. Annual Requirements and Taxes

   No annual filing requirements.

7. Licenses and Permits

   Varies based on location and type of business.

# MONTANA

1. Name Reservation

   Name Search:

   https://www.mtsosfilings.gov/mtsos-master/service/create.html?service=registerItemSearch

   **Must end in one of the following designators:**
   - ☐ LLC
   - ☐ L.L.C.
   - ☐ Limited Liability Company
   - ☐ LC
   - ☐ L.C.
   - ☐ Limited Company
   - ☐ Ltd. Liability Company
   - ☐ Ltd. Liability Co.
   - ☐ Limited Liability Company
   - ☐ Limited Liability Co.

   Cannot end in any of the following designators:
   - ☐ Corporation
   - ☐ Incorporated
   - ☐ Corp.
   - ☐ Inc.
   - ☐ Cooperative
   - ☐ Limited Partnership

- ☐ LP
- ☐ L.P.
- ☐ Ltd.
- ☐ Limited Liability Partnership
- ☐ LLP
- ☐ L.L.P.

2. Registered Agent

   Required in the state of Montana

3. Filing Forms and Fees
   - $70
   - Filed with Secretary of State
   - File online: https://www.mtsosfilings.gov

4. Operating Agreements and Publishing Requirements

   No required but recommended.

   No publishing requirements.

5. Tax ID Number (EIN)

   Through the IRS online or by mail with Form SS-4: https://sa.www4.irs.gov/modiein/individual/index.jsp

6. Annual Requirements and Taxes
   - Annual Report must be filed each year.
   - Filed with Secretary of State.
   - Costs $20
   - Due before April 15th of every year.

7. Licenses and Permits

   Varies based on location and type of business.

# NEBRASKA

1. Name Reservation

    Name Search:

    https://www.nebraska.gov/sos/corp/corpsearch.cgi?nav=search

    Must end in one of the following designators:
    - ☐ LLC
    - ☐ L.L.C.

    Cannot end in any of the following designators:
    - ☐ Corporation
    - ☐ Incorporated
    - ☐ Corp.
    - ☐ Inc.

2. Registered Agent

    Required in the state of Nebraska

3. Filing Forms and Fees
    - $105
    - Filed with Secretary of State

4. Operating Agreements and Publishing Requirements

    Not required, but recommended.

    Must publish a notice of organization for 3 consecutive weeks in a newspaper of general circulation in the county the business is located.

5. Tax ID Number (EIN)

   Through the IRS online or by mail with Form SS-4: https://sa.www4.irs.gov/modiein/individual/index.jsp

6. Annual Requirements and Taxes
   - Biennial Report must be filed every 2 years.
   - Filed with Secretary of State.
   - Costs $13
   - Due between January 1st and April 1st in odd-numbered years.

7. Licenses and Permits

   Varies based on location and type of business.

# NEVADA

1. Name Reservation

    Name Search:

    https://www.nvsos.gov/sosentitysearch/

    Must end in one of the following designators:
    - ☐ LLC
    - ☐ L.L.C.
    - ☐ Limited-Liability Company
    - ☐ Limited Liability Company
    - ☐ Limited Company
    - ☐ Limited
    - ☐ Ltd.
    - ☐ LC

2. Registered Agent

    Required in the state of Nevada

3. Filing Forms and Fees
    - $75
    - Filed with Secretary of State

4. Operating Agreements and Publishing Requirements

    Not required, but recommended.

    No publishing requirements.

5. Tax ID Number (EIN)

    Through the IRS online or by mail with Form SS-4:

https://sa.www4.irs.gov/modiein/individual/index.jsp

6. Annual Requirements and Taxes
   - Must file Annual Reports every year.
   - Due by the last day of the anniversary month.
   - Costs $150
   - Filed with Secretary of State
7. Licenses and Permits

   Varies based on location and type of business.

# NEW HAMPSHIRE

1. Name Reservation

    Name Search:

    https://quickstart.sos.nh.gov/online/BusinessInquire

    Must end with one of the following designators:
    - ☐ LLC
    - ☐ L.L.C.

    Cannot end with any of the following designators:
    - ☐ Corporation
    - ☐ Incorporated
    - ☐ Corp.
    - ☐ Inc.

2. Registered Agent

    Required in the state of New Hampshire

3. Filing Forms and Fees
    - $100
    - Filed with Secretary of State
    - Form LLC-1:

        http://sos.nh.gov/WorkArea/DownloadAsset.aspx?id=8589958994

4. Operating Agreements and Publishing Requirements

Not required, but recommended.

No publishing requirements.

5. Tax ID Number (EIN)

    Through the IRS online or by mail with Form SS-4: https://sa.www4.irs.gov/modiein/individual/index.jsp

6. Annual Requirements and Taxes
    - Annual Report must be filed every year.
    - Costs $102
    - Due between January 1st and April 1st each year.
    - Filed with Corporation Division

7. Licenses and Permits

    Varies based on location and type of business.

# NEW JERSEY

1. Name Reservation

    Name Search:

    https://www.njportal.com/DOR/BusinessNameSearch/Search/Availability

    Must end in one of the following designators:
    - ☐ LLC
    - ☐ L.L.C.

2. Registered Agent

    Required in the state of New Jersey

3. Filing Forms and Fees
    - $125
    - Filed with the Department of Treasury, Division of Revenue and Enterprise Services

4. Operating Agreements and Publishing Requirements

    Not required, but recommended.

    No publishing requirements.

5. Tax ID Number (EIN)

    Through the IRS online or by mail with Form SS-4:

    https://sa.www4.irs.gov/modiein/individual/index.jsp

6. Annual Requirements and Taxes
    - Annual Report must be filed each year.

- Due on the anniversary month.
- Filed with Division of Revenue.
- Costs $50

7. Licenses and Permits

Varies based on location and type of business.

# NEW MEXICO

1. Name Reservation

    Name Search:

    https://portal.sos.state.nm.us/BFS/online/CorporationBusinessSearch

    Must end with one of the following designators:
    - ☐ LLC
    - ☐ L.L.C.

    Cannot end with any of the following designators:
    - ☐ Corporation
    - ☐ Incorporated
    - ☐ Corp.
    - ☐ Inc.

2. Registered Agent

    Required in the state of New Mexico

3. Filing Forms and Fees
    - $50
    - Form:

    http://www.sos.state.nm.us/uploads/files/dllc.pdf

    - Filed with Secretary of State

4. Operating Agreements and Publishing Requirements

   Not required, but recommended.

   No publishing requirements.

5. Tax ID Number (EIN)

   Through the IRS online or by mail with Form SS-4: https://sa.www4.irs.gov/modiein/individual/index.jsp

6. Annual Requirements and Taxes

   No annual filing requirements

7. Licenses and Permits

   Varies based on location and type of business.

# NEW YORK

1. Name Reservation

   Name Search:

   https://appext20.dos.ny.gov/corp_public/CORPSEARCH.ENTITY_SEARCH_ENTRY

2. Registered Agent

   Required in the state of New York

3. Filing Forms and Fees
   - $200
   - Filed with the Department of State
   - File online:

     http://www.dos.ny.gov/corps/index.html

4. Operating Agreements and Publishing Requirements

   An operating agreement is required in the state of New York.

   Within 120 days of filing, an LLC must publish a copy of the articles or a notice of formation in two newspapers in the county that the business is located.

5. Tax ID Number (EIN)

   Through the IRS online or by mail with Form SS-4:

   https://sa.www4.irs.gov/modiein/individual/index.jsp

6. Annual Requirements and Taxes

No annual filings required
7. Licenses and Permits

   Varies based on location and type of business.

# NORTH CAROLINA

1. Name Reservation

    Name Search:

    http://www.sosnc.gov/search/index/corp

    Must end with one of the following designators:
    - ☐ LLC
    - ☐ L.L.C.
    - ☐ Limited Liability Company
    - ☐ Limited Liability Co.
    - ☐ Ltd. Liability Company
    - ☐ Ltd. Liability Co.

    Cannot end with any of the following designators:
    - ☐ Corporation
    - ☐ Incorporated
    - ☐ Corp.
    - ☐ Inc.
    - ☐ Limited Partnership
    - ☐ LP
    - ☐ L.P.
    - ☐ Trust

2. Registered Agent

    Required in the state of North Carolina

3. Filing Forms and Fees
    - $125

- Filed with Secretary of State
4. Operating Agreements and Publishing Requirements

   Not required, but recommended.

   No publishing requirements.

5. Tax ID Number (EIN)

   Through the IRS online or by mail with Form SS-4: https://sa.www4.irs.gov/modiein/individual/index.jsp

6. Annual Requirements and Taxes
   - Annual Report must be filed every year.
   - Due by April 15th of each year.
   - Costs $200
   - Filed with Secretary of State

7. Licenses and Permits

   Varies based on location and type of business.

# NORTH DAKOTA

1. Name Reservation

   Name Search:

   https://apps.nd.gov/sc/busnsrch/busnSearch.htm

   Must end with one of the following designators:
   - ☐ LLC
   - ☐ L.L.C.

   Cannot end with any of the following designators:
   - ☐ Corporation
   - ☐ Incorporated
   - ☐ Corp.
   - ☐ Inc.

2. Registered Agent

   Required in the state of North Dakota

3. Filing Forms and Fees
   - $135
   - Form SFN58701:

   http://www.nd.gov/eforms/Doc/sfn58701.pdf
   - File with Secretary of State

4. Operating Agreements and Publishing Requirements

   Not required, but recommended.

No publishing requirements.

5. Tax ID Number (EIN)

   Through the IRS online or by mail with Form SS-4: https://sa.www4.irs.gov/modiein/individual/index.jsp

6. Annual Requirements and Taxes
   - Must file an Annual Report every year.
   - Costs $50
   - Due by November 15th each year.
   - Filed with Secretary of State

7. Licenses and Permits

   Varies based on location and type of business.

# OHIO

1. Name Reservation

    Name Search:

    https://www5.sos.state.oh.us/ords/f?p=100:1

    Must end with one of the following designators:
    - LLC
    - L.L.C.
    - Ltd.
    - Limited
    - Limited Liability Company

    Cannot end in any of the following designators:
    - Corporation
    - Incorporated
    - Corp.
    - Inc.
    - Limited Partnership
    - LP
    - L.P.
    - Trust

2. Registered Agent

    Required in the state of Ohio

3. Filing Forms and Fees
    - $99
    - Form 533A

- File online: https://bsportal.sos.state.oh.us/default.aspx
- Filed with Secretary of State
4. Operating Agreement and Publishing Requirements

   Not required, but recommended.

   No publishing requirements.
5. Tax ID Number (EIN)

   Through the IRS online or by mail with Form SS-4: https://sa.www4.irs.gov/modiein/individual/index.jsp
6. Annual Requirements and Taxes

   No annual filing requirements.
7. Licenses and Permits

   Varies depending on location and type of business.

# OKLAHOMA

1. Name Reservation

    Name Search:

    https://www.sos.ok.gov/business/corp/records.aspx

    Must end in one of the following designators:
    - LLC
    - L.L.C.

    Cannot end with any of the following designators:
    - Corporation
    - Incorporated
    - Corp.
    - Inc.

2. Registered Agent

    Required in the state of Oklahoma

3. Filing Forms and Fees
    - $100
    - Form:

    https://www.sos.ok.gov/forms/FM0074.PDF
    - Filed with Secretary of State

4. Operating Agreement and Publishing Requirements

    Not required, but recommended.

No publishing requirements.

5. Tax ID Number (EIN)

   Through the IRS online or by mail with Form SS-4:

   https://sa.www4.irs.gov/modiein/individual/index.jsp

6. Annual Requirements and Taxes
   - File an Annual Certificate every year.
   - Costs $25
   - Due by the anniversary date.
   - Filed with Secretary of State
   - Form:

   https://www.sos.ok.gov/forms/LLCAnnualCertificate.pdf

7. Licenses and Permits

   Varies based on location and type of business.

# OREGON

1. Name Reservation

   Name Search:

   http://egov.sos.state.or.us/br/pkg_web_name_srch_inq.login

   Must end with one of the following designators:
   - ☐ LLC
   - ☐ L.L.C.
   - ☐ Limited Liability Company

   Cannot end with any of the following designators:
   - ☐ Corporation
   - ☐ Incorporated
   - ☐ Corp.
   - ☐ Inc.
   - ☐ Limited Partnership
   - ☐ LP
   - ☐ L.P.
   - ☐ Trust

2. Registered Agent

   Required in the state of Oregon

3. Filing Forms and Fees
   - $100
   - Form:

     http://sos.oregon.gov/business/Do

cuments/business-registry-forms/llc-articles.pdf
- Filed with Secretary of State
- File online: http://egov.sos.state.or.us/br/pkg_br1_web_rnewl.login

4. Operating Agreement and Publishing Requirements

   Not required, but recommended.

   No publishing requirements.

5. Tax ID Number (EIN)

   Through the IRS online or by mail with Form SS-4: https://sa.www4.irs.gov/modiein/individual/index.jsp

6. Annual Requirements and Taxes
   - Annual Report must be filed every year.
   - Costs $100
   - Due by the anniversary date.
   - Filed with Secretary of State
   - File online: http://egov.sos.state.or.us/br/pkg_br1_web_rnewl.login

7. Licenses and Permits

   Varies based on location and type of business.

# PENNSYLVANIA

1. Name Reservation

   Name Search:

   https://www.corporations.pa.gov/search/corpsearch

   Must end with one of the following designators:
   - ☐ LLC
   - ☐ L.L.C.
   - ☐ LTD
   - ☐ Ltd.
   - ☐ Limited Liability Company
   - ☐ Limited Liability Co.
   - ☐ Ltd. Liability Company
   - ☐ Ltd. Liability Co.
   - ☐ Limited
   - ☐ Company
   - ☐ Co.

2. Registered Agent

   Required in the state of Pennsylvania

3. Filing Forms and Fees
   - $125
   - Filed with the Department of State

- File online: https://www.corporations.pa.gov/Account/Register_account
4. Operating Agreement and Publishing Requirements

    Not required, but recommended.

    No publishing requirements.
5. Tax ID Number (EIN)

    Through the IRS online or by mail with Form SS-4: https://sa.www4.irs.gov/modiein/individual/index.jsp
6. Annual Requirements and Taxes
    - Requires Decennial Reports, once every 10 years.
    - Due on years ending in 1.
7. Licenses and Permits

    Varies based on location and type of business.

# RHODE ISLAND

1. Name Reservation

    Name Search:

    http://ucc.state.ri.us/CorpSearch/CorpSearchInput.asp

    Must end with one of the following designators:
    - LLC
    - L.L.C.

    Cannot end with any of the following designators:
    - Corporation
    - Incorporated
    - Corp.
    - Inc.

2. Registered Agent

    Required in the state of Rhode Island

3. Filing Forms and Fees
    - $150
    - Form 400:

        http://www.sos.ri.gov/assets/downloads/documents/400-articles-of-organization.pdf
    - Filed with Division of Business Services

- File online: http://ucc.state.ri.us/loginsystem/login_form.asp

4. Operating Agreement and Publishing Requirements

   Not required, but recommended.

   No publishing requirements.

5. Tax ID Number (EIN)

   Through the IRS online or by mail with Form SS-4: https://sa.www4.irs.gov/modiein/individual/index.jsp

6. Annual Requirements and Taxes
   - Annual Report required each year.
   - Costs $50
   - Filed with Division of Business Services
   - Due between September 1st and November 1st of each year.
   - Form 632: http://sos.ri.gov/assets/downloads/documents/632-limited-liability-company-annual-report.pdf

7. Licenses and Permits

   Varies based on location and type of business.

# SOUTH CAROLINA

1. Name Reservation

   Name Search:

   https://businessfilings.sc.gov/BusinessFiling/Entity/Search

   Must end in one of the following designators:
   - ☐ LLC
   - ☐ L.L.C.
   - ☐ LC
   - ☐ L.C.
   - ☐ Ltd. Liability Co.
   - ☐ Limited Liability Co.
   - ☐ Ltd. Liability Company
   - ☐ Limited Liability Company

   Cannot end with any of the following designators:
   - ☐ Corporation
   - ☐ Incorporated
   - ☐ Corp.
   - ☐ Inc.
   - ☐ Limited Partnership
   - ☐ LP
   - ☐ L.P.
   - ☐ Trust

2. Registered Agent

Required in the state of South Carolina
3. Filing Forms and Fees
    - $110
    - Form: http://www.sos.sc.gov/forms/LLC/Domestic/ArticlesofOrganization.pdf
    - File online: https://businessfilings.sc.gov/BusinessFiling/Account/Register
    - Filed with Secretary of State
4. Operating Agreement and Publishing Requirements

    Not required, but recommended.

    No publishing requirements.
5. Tax ID Number (EIN)

    Through the IRS online or by mail with Form SS-4: https://sa.www4.irs.gov/modiein/individual/index.jsp
6. Annual Requirements and Taxes

    No annual filing required.
7. Licenses and Permits

    Varies based on location and type of business.

# SOUTH DAKOTA

1. Name Reservation

   Name Search:

   https://sosenterprise.sd.gov/BusinessServices/Business/FilingSearch.aspx

   Must end in one of the following designators:
   - ☐ LC
   - ☐ L.C.
   - ☐ LLC
   - ☐ L.L.C.
   - ☐ Ltd. Liability Co.
   - ☐ Ltd. Liability Company
   - ☐ Limited Liability Co.
   - ☐ Limited Liability Company

   Cannot use any of the following designators:
   - ☐ Corporation
   - ☐ Incorporated
   - ☐ Corp.
   - ☐ Inc.
   - ☐ Limited Partnership
   - ☐ LP
   - ☐ L.P.
   - ☐ Trust

2. Registered Agent

Required in the state of South Dakota
3. Filing Forms and Fees
    - $150
    - Form: https://sdsos.gov/docs/business/domesticllcarticlesoforganization20180215.pdf
    - File online: https://sosenterprise.sd.gov/BusinessServices/Business/RegistrationInstr.aspx
    - Filed with Secretary of State
4. Operating Agreement and Publishing Requirements

    Not required, but recommended.

    No publishing requirements.
5. Tax ID Number (EIN)

    Through the IRS online or by mail with Form SS-4: https://sa.www4.irs.gov/modiein/individual/index.jsp
6. Annual Requirements and Taxes
    - Must file an Annual Report every year.
    - Costs $65
    - Due by the last day of anniversary month.

- Form: https://sdsos.gov/docs/business/domesticllcannualreport20180215.pdf
- File online: https://sosenterprise.sd.gov/BusinessServices/Business/AnnualReportInstr.aspx
- Filed with Secretary of State

7. Licenses and Permits

Varies based on location and type of business.

# TENNESSEE

1. Name Reservation

    Name Search:

    https://tnbear.tn.gov/Ecommerce/NameAvailability.aspx

2. Registered Agent

    Required in the state of Tennessee

3. Filing Forms and Fees
    - $300
    - Filed with Secretary of State

4. Operating Agreement and Publishing Requirements

    Not required, but recommended.

    No publishing requirements.

5. Tax ID Number (EIN)

    Through the IRS online or by mail with Form SS-4:

    https://sa.www4.irs.gov/modiein/individual/index.jsp

6. Annual Requirements and Taxes
    - Annual Report is due each year.
    - Costs $300
    - Due by the 1st day of the 4th month after the end of the business's fiscal year.
    - Filed with Secretary of State

- File online:
  
  https://tnbear.tn.gov/Ecommerce/AnnualReportInstr.aspx

7. Licenses and Permits

   Varies based on location and type of business.

# TEXAS

1. Name Reservation

   Name Search:

   https://mycpa.cpa.state.tx.us/coa/

   Must end with one of the following designators:
   - ☐ LLC
   - ☐ L.L.C.
   - ☐ Limited Liability Company
   - ☐ Limited Liability Co.
   - ☐ Ltd. Liability Company
   - ☐ Ltd. Liability Co.
   - ☐ Limited Company
   - ☐ Ltd.
   - ☐ Co.
   - ☐ Limited Co.

2. Registered Agent

   Required in the state of Tennessee

3. Filing Forms and Fees
   - $300
   - Form 205 and 401A
   - File online:

     https://direct.sos.state.tx.us/acct/acct-login.asp
   - Filed with Corporations Section

4. Operating Agreement and Publishing Requirements

   Not required, but recommended.

   No publishing requirements.

5. Tax ID Number (EIN)

   Through the IRS online or by mail with Form SS-4: https://sa.www4.irs.gov/modiein/individual/index.jsp

6. Annual Requirements and Taxes

   No annual filing requirements.

7. Licenses and Permits

   Varies based on location and type of business.

# UTAH

1. Name Reservation

    Name Search:

    https://secure.utah.gov/bes/

    Must end with one of the following designators:
    - ☐ LLC
    - ☐ L.L.C.
    - ☐ LC
    - ☐ L.C.
    - ☐ Limited Liability Company
    - ☐ Limited Company

2. Registered Agent

    Required in the state of Utah

3. Filing Forms and Fees
    - $70
    - Filed with Division of Corporations
    - File online:

        https://secure.utah.gov/account/log-in.html

4. Operating Agreement and Publishing Requirements

    Not required, but recommended.

    No publishing requirements.

5. Tax ID Number (EIN)

Through the IRS online or by mail with Form SS-4: https://sa.www4.irs.gov/modiein/individual/index.jsp

6. Annual Requirements and Taxes
   - Annual Renewal required each year.
   - Costs $15
   - Filed with the Division of Corporations.
   - Due on the anniversary date.
7. Licenses and Permits

   Varies based on location and type of business.

# VERMONT

1. Name Reservation

   Name Search:

   https://www.vtsosonline.com/online/BusinessInquire/

   Must end with one of the following designators:
   - LLC
   - L.L.C.
   - LC
   - L.C.
   - Ltd. Liability Co.
   - Ltd. Liability Company
   - Limited Liability Co.
   - Limited Liability Company

2. Registered Agent

   Required in the state of Vermont

3. Filing Forms and Fees
   - $125
   - Form LLC-1 D

     https://www.sec.state.vt.us/media/537849/llc-1-d-_domestic_reg.pdf

- File online:
  https://www.vtsosonline.com/online/Account
- Filed with Secretary of State

4. Operating Agreement and Publishing Requirements

   Not required, but recommended.

   No publishing requirements.

5. Tax ID Number (EIN)

   Through the IRS online or by mail with Form SS-4: https://sa.www4.irs.gov/modiein/individual/index.jsp

6. Annual Requirements and Taxes
   - Annual Report must be filed every year.
   - Costs $35
   - Due between January 1st and March 31st of each year.
   - Filed with Secretary of State

7. Licenses and Permits

   Varies based on location and type of business.

# VIRGINIA

1. Name Reservation

    Name Search: https://sccefile.scc.virginia.gov/NameAvailability

2. Registered Agent

    Required in the state of Virginia

3. Filing Forms and Fees
    - $100
    - Filed with Clerk of the State, Corporation Commission

4. Operating Agreement and Publishing Requirements

    Not required, but recommended.

    No publishing requirements.

5. Tax ID Number (EIN)

    Through the IRS online or by mail with Form SS-4: https://sa.www4.irs.gov/modiein/individual/index.jsp

6. Annual Requirements and Taxes
    - Pay annual registration fee of $50
    - Due by the last day of the business anniversary month

7. Licenses and Permits

Varies based on location and type of business.

# WASHINGTON

1. Name Reservation

    Name Search:

    https://www.sos.wa.gov/corps/

    Must end in one of the following designators:
    - ☐ LLC
    - ☐ L.L.C.
    - ☐ Limited Liability Co.
    - ☐ Limited Liability Company

2. Registered Agent

    Required in the state of Washington

3. Filing Forms and Fees
    - $180
    - Filed with Secretary of State

4. Operating Agreement and Publishing Requirements

    Not required, but recommended.

    No publishing requirements.

5. Tax ID Number (EIN)

    Through the IRS online or by mail with Form SS-4:

    https://sa.www4.irs.gov/modiein/individual/index.jsp

6. Annual Requirements and Taxes
    - Must file an Annual Report each year.

- Filed with Secretary of State.
- The initial report filed within 120 days of formation.
- Annual dates determined by Secretary of State.
- Costs $71

7. Licenses and Permits

   Varies based on location and type of business.

# WEST VIRGINIA

1. Name Reservation

   Name Search:

   http://apps.sos.wv.gov/business/corporations/

   Must end with one of the following designators:
   - ☐ LLC
   - ☐ L.L.C.
   - ☐ LC
   - ☐ L.C.
   - ☐ Limited Liability Company
   - ☐ Limited Company

2. Registered Agent

   Required in the state of West Virginia

3. Filing Forms and Fees
   - $100
   - Form LLD-1
   - Filed with Secretary of State

4. Operating Agreements and Publishing Requirements

   Not required, but recommended.

   No publishing requirements.

5. Tax ID Number (EIN)

   Through the IRS online or by mail with Form SS-4:

https://sa.www4.irs.gov/modiein/individual/index.jsp

6. Annual Requirements and Taxes
    - File an Annual Report each year.
    - Filed with Secretary of State.
    - Costs $25.
    - Due between January 1st and June 30th of each year.
7. Licenses and Permits

    Varies based on location and type of business.

# WISCONSIN

1. Name Reservation

    Name Search:

    https://www.wdfi.org/apps/CorpSearch/NameAvailability.aspx

    Must end in one of the following designators:
    - ☐ LLC
    - ☐ L.L.C.
    - ☐ Limited Liability Company
    - ☐ Limited Liability Co.

2. Registered Agent

    Required in the state of Wisconsin

3. Filing Forms and Fees
    - $130
    - Form 502
    - Filed with the Department of Financial Institutions

4. Operating Agreements and Publishing Requirements

    Not required, but recommended.

    No publishing requirements.

5. Tax ID Number (EIN)

    Through the IRS online or by mail with Form SS-4:

https://sa.www4.irs.gov/modiein/individual/index.jsp

6. Annual Requirements and Taxes
   - Annual Report due each year.
   - Filed with the Department of Financial Institutions
   - Due at the end of the calendar year of the anniversary date
   - Costs $25
7. Licenses and Permits

   Varies based on location and type of business.

# WYOMING

1. Name Reservation

    Name Search:

    https://wyobiz.wy.gov/business/filingsearch.aspx

    Must end with one of the following designators:
    - ☐ LLC
    - ☐ L.L.C.
    - ☐ LC
    - ☐ L.C.
    - ☐ Ltd.
    - ☐ LTD.
    - ☐ Limited Company
    - ☐ Liability Company
    - ☐ Ltd. Liability Co.
    - ☐ Limited Liability Co.
    - ☐ Limited Liability Company

    Cannot end with any of the following designators:
    - ☐ Corporation
    - ☐ Incorporated
    - ☐ Corp.
    - ☐ Inc.
    - ☐ Limited Partnership
    - ☐ LP

- ☐ L.P.
- ☐ Trust

2. Registered Agent

   Required in the state of Wyoming

3. Filing Forms and Fees
   - $100
   - Form: https://soswy.state.wy.us/Forms/Business/LLC/LLC-ArticlesOrganization.pdf
   - File online: https://wyobiz.wy.gov/Business/RegistrationInstr.aspx
   - Filed with Secretary of State

4. Operating Agreements and Publishing Requirements

   Not required, but recommended.

   No publishing requirements.

5. Tax ID Number (EIN)

   Through the IRS online or by mail with Form SS-4: https://sa.www4.irs.gov/modiein/individual/index.jsp

6. Annual Requirements and Taxes
   - Annual Report due each year.
   - Costs $50.

- Due first day of the formation month.

7. Licenses and Permits

   Varies based on location and type of business.

# CONCLUSION

As you can see, there isn't that much involved in starting and running an LLC. It is more about doing it right the first time, so you do not have to go back and refile any documents. This will save you time, money and most importantly a lot of unnecessary headaches.

Last but not the least, I want to say THANK YOU for purchasing and reading this book. I really hope you got a lot out of it! Despite our best efforts, if you found any errors or typos in my work, please forgive me as this was my second try at writing such guides, I promise I will get better.

Can I ask you for a quick favor though?

If you enjoyed this book, I would really appreciate it if you could leave me a Review.

I LOVE getting feedback from my wonderful readers, and reviews really do make the difference. I read all of my reviews and would love to hear your thoughts.

Thank you and God Bless.